The
Secret
Life of
HENRY
FORD

The
Secret
Life of
HENRY
FORD

by
John Côté
Dahlinger
as told to Frances Spatz Leighton

The Bobbs-Merrill Company, Inc.
Indianapolis/New York

Designed by Jacques Chazaud
Manufactured in the United States of America

First printing

Library of Congress Cataloging in Publication Data
Dahlinger, John.
    The secret life of Henry Ford.
    1. Ford, Henry, 1863–1947. 2. Businessmen—United
States—Biography. I. Leighton, Frances Spatz, joint
author. II. Title.
HD9710.U52F663   629.2'092'4 [B]   77–15422
ISBN 0–672–52377–9

With love to my wife,
Bette

I am indebted to writer Hurley Hayes McAllister for the skillful work in helping to compile information, for the time devoted in reading and editing the typescript, and for the endless research.

Also a special thank you to Mary Jane Gneuhs for helping me in countless ways. Her assistance with the editing was invaluable.

And a thank you to Roland Marquardt.

J.C.D.
1978

Table
of Contents

The
Secret
Life of
HENRY
FORD

1
The Secret Life of Henry Ford

I grew up close to a famous man whom I called Mister. I am satisfied in my own mind that I am his child.

I had a legal father whom I called Dad.

I had a mother who shared her life with both men in a style that would have made a great soap opera had the truth been known. Or a great novel.

I had a half-brother. His name was Edsel Ford.

Yes, the man in all our lives—the man who dominated my family, me, and his son, Edsel, until Edsel's tragic death—was Henry Ford.

Why am I telling this now? For many reasons. And for the fact that a Ford biographer has finally put it into writing—nobody has ever before stated it in black and white. David L. Lewis, a highly respected professor of business history at the University of Michigan, spent nineteen years researching his 600-page book, *The Public Image of Henry Ford*. In his introduction, Lewis notes (p. 12):

"He shunned the conventional vices, although circumstantial evidence suggests that he had a brief, intense extramarital relationship during the early 1920s."

I was born in 1923. Lewis tried to contact Mother; when he learned she was elderly and incapacitated, he wanted to talk to me—but I carefully avoided seeing him.

Now he will understand why. I have finally decided to tell my own story. Not just because of what Lewis wrote, but because I am a little tired of having the Dahlingers swept under the rug, as it were. It is hard to say exactly what I feel—a little anger, a little pride, and a little concern with history, and setting the record straight. Yes, I am now serene enough to tell the truth as I know it: that I am Henry Ford's son.

It took the mellowing of years for me to reach the stage where I can admit my probable illegitimacy for all the world to see. I still cling to the word *probable*, because I was not there to witness my inception.

I was born in an era of high moral principles, snobbishness, and hypocrisy. My mother was a proud woman, and having this fact made public would have killed her, as the saying goes.

It was not something we talked about—or could talk about. When everyone else seemed to know it but me, I finally confronted her and she confirmed it; not by admitting it, but by not denying it.

My mother, Evangeline Dahlinger, is still a proud woman, but now ill and elderly, and Henry Ford is something that happened a long time ago—I am fifty-five now. This is a story of other places and other moods.

It is a story of strange intensities and pettiness. It is a story of wealth that boggles my mind, even now, as I recall how casually I knew and accepted the fact that there was a million dollars in cash hidden in a certain place. I knew the place. It would not have entered my mind to help myself to it.

I was part of that world of wealth in which the strange old man dwelt, and early on I had more things than I could think of, let alone want. Henry Ford was determined that I would have the same treatment as his own grandchildren, who were about my age and were my playmates. In making sure that I was equal, he heaped toys and material wealth upon me.

I was part of a world so strange that even now I am working to truly understand it; perhaps I will never understand it all. I was part of the secret life of Henry Ford, sheltered, protected by bodyguards, raised by a nanny who took care of me while my mother was out and around doing many things for the Ford Motor Company, Mr. Ford himself, the Ford family, and even Mrs. Ford. In a way, she did what she wanted to, and in another way she did whatever Ford wanted her to do.

To know the secret life of Henry Ford, you would have to know Evangeline, my mother. And you would have to know all of Ford's unusual relationships with the people who made up his world—mainly people connected in some way with motor cars and the Ford Motor Company.

You will, before we are through, know them all, as I knew them. If it all seems a little odd, I can't help it; it's the way I lived. Ford was not at all the man who steps forth from the stuffy pages of a history book. He was many conflicting things, sometimes rigid, sometimes changeable, sometimes predictable— but usually not.

When he died, my mother and I were the first ones to be called. Our property adjoined his. This wasn't accidental; he had given it to us. Yet, as soon as possible, all traces of the Dahlinger family were, in effect, wiped from the record. That's where my anger comes in. Why do I write? Because the Ford family has taken such pains to erase my family's name from history.

Had they been gracious, I would probably have been content to stay in the shadows, with just the dignified cards in the Henry Ford Museum testifying that Evangeline and Ray Dahlinger once lived and that they spent their working lives with the Fords and contributed these many objects and artifacts to the display.

There were so many things that the Henry Ford Museum asked for and received from the Dahlingers, and others that we volunteered to contribute, to illustrate Henry Ford's life style, tastes, personality, and inventiveness.

For example, there is the special car in which Dad drove Henry Ford around during the last years of his life. It does not have a plaque showing that it came from Ray Dahlinger; and there are other things.

My contribution of a Model A convertible does not bear my name. It was my prize possession, a 1931 or '32 model with a rumble seat. My name is not mentioned anywhere in connection with this car, or to my knowledge anywhere in the Henry Ford Museum.

In the Henry Ford Museum each exhibit is accompanied by a placard giving the name of the donor and vital information about the object. Mother and Dad donated dozens of important artifacts and not once is a placard found beside our donations. Why?

I am happy to say that we did not give everything to the museum that Ford had given us. We did not give his christening gown, for example, which was the gown in which I was christened. There is a little tractor which I still have that Henry Ford made especially for me. And the museum did not get a little car in which I used to ride up and down the roads at age six.

When I visited the museum recently, I laughed when I saw an exhibit of what was claimed to be Henry Ford's baby bed. It certainly is not, because I have his baby bed. It's the bed that I slept in and that Henry Ford gave my mother when I was born, telling her that it had been his.

He wanted me to sleep in his bed. He wanted me, he told her—and hinted to me—to grow up to walk in his footsteps.

It's too late to walk in his footsteps. I was too stubborn and independent while he lived even to make a start at walking in his footsteps. But it is not too late to clear the air and tell the truth.

As mother's health and memory faded and I took over the management of her affairs, I found many mementos from the past, the dreams she had lived on since Henry Ford's death in

1947. Secreted in out-of-the-way places were diaries she had kept when her greatest joy was keeping up with the Boss, as she called him. She had kept my little fancy gloves, worn when I was only three or four. "What in the world are they for?" asked my wife in surprise as we looked over the house together.

"Oh, didn't I tell you?" I said. "I wasn't permitted to get my hands dirty when I fooled around with machinery, for fear of injury." In one photo I have, I am holding up a mouse with those little gloves, a mouse that I'd found in the threshing machine. Little Henry II is standing behind me.

My earliest recollection of the man who, I am sure in my own mind, was my father is of his putting me on his foot, crossing his legs and giving me a horsey ride. I remember, young as I was, that he was not laughing out loud, only smiling as he did it.

I realized he didn't laugh a lot, like the other people who played with me—Mother, the gardener, my nanny, or the man I called Dad.

When I was four or five, Henry Ford bought me a car. I have a picture of it. I believe it was from England. It was a little car for a little person. It ran with a motor and must have gone all of five to ten miles per hour—faster than a tricycle.

A few years later, when I was six or seven, Ford gave me the racing car that had finished fifth at the 1923 Indy race—the Fronty Ford race car.

When he gave me the Fronty, Ford said, "The only reason I'm letting you have this racer is that you did so well with your first little car."

I looked at it wide-eyed. "But how can I drive it?" I said, all excited. "I'll have to wait till I'm big."

"Oh no you won't," he said with a little smile, and took me over to the car. Inside was a special bucket seat and other adjustments so I could reach the pedals.

Delirious with joy, I drove the Indianapolis race car endlessly around and around the half-mile horse track on our farm. My nanny could hardly get me home for dinner. She had to flag me down.

Though Ford gave many gifts and received many gifts, he himself walked around completely unadorned. He did not even wear a wedding ring that I recall. The only cuff links he would wear were simple functional ones. He did have a watch, but that was something functional too. He wore it on a fob, tucked away in his watch pocket.

The only other thing he carried was something I had given him—a jackknife—and he seemed to cherish it. He would take it out on any pretext and fiddle with it or cut some leather strand or thread. Or he would whack a branch and start whittling.

Though Henry Ford received an endless supply of shaving creams and after-shave preparations, I don't remember his ever smelling of cologne or lotion. He was a firm believer in soap and water, and didn't want me to use "sissy things."

As for his clothes, if you were going to bet what color he'd be wearing, it was a safe bet that it would be some shade of gray. He was a study in gray; he could have posed for Whistler's father.

His hair was gray; he was sixty years old when I was born, so I knew him only as a gray-haired man. His eyes were gray. His suits were gray. He wore a gray hat. He even lived in a gray house. He rode around in a conservative car. He used ordinary Ford cars. Mrs. Ford used fancier cars—chauffeured Lincoln limousines.

When he came to our house, he would take off his coat but would not open his shirt—perhaps the age lines on his neck bothered him. He was very sensitive about his age and wanted to show how young he was in action. He would take large stair steps two at a time.

I have a picture he gave Mother of a time he went camping with his special buddies: Thomas Edison; John Burroughs, the naturalist; and Harvey Firestone, Sr., the tire king; and even here his collar was not open.

At our house he went around with his shirt collar buttoned. He wore high collars that came tight to his chin, and they were stiffly starched and immaculate.

Ford never had his nails polished, and he had only contempt

for men who did. His handshake was very nice, very firm. It inspired trust instantly. I can count on one hand the times I remember Ford showing his affection by hugging me.

Instead, he would shake hands with me, even when I was a little boy. Frequently he would pat me on the head. Often he would sit right up against me, on a stump or a log. We'd stop and rest, and he'd pull out his jew's harp and I'd pull out mine, and we'd pluck away in close harmony—if such a thing is possible.

I forgot to mention Ford's shoes. He had a horror of fancy footwear. He never wore loafers. He had his shoes made in the Village by the cobbler. I would sometimes go with him when he went to order another pair of very plain black shoes.

Ford's pocket knife was involved in an incident that I will never forget and through which he taught me a memorable lesson. When I was about ten, Mother and I went shopping for my present for Henry Ford on his birthday, which must have been about his seventieth.

I saw a pocket knife with a carved cherrywood jacket and I loved it. I really wanted it for myself, but I realized I had to give it to Mr. Ford. Never did I covet something the way I wanted that knife. It did not occur to me to buy two of them, one for him and one for me. For one thing, Mother would have disapproved of such half-hearted gift giving; and, besides, there was only one such elegant knife in the display case.

When I gave my gift to Mr. Ford, I said—as only a child can, and hoping my mother wouldn't hear me—"Happy birthday. If you ever decide you don't want this anymore, could I please have it back?"

Ford looked the slightest bit startled and cracked a grin as he said, "I'll remember that, John." I looked around and was relieved to see that Mother had not heard, for in a flash I knew that what I had done was dead wrong.

Years later, when I was leaving to go into the service during World War II, Ford handed me a package and said, "If you ever decide you don't want this, will you please give it back?"

I carried that same little knife through the service and gave it back when I returned. When Ford died, the little knife was in his pocket.

Gone, gone. All of that is gone. What remains is memory and the pain of seeing others trying to erase that memory. It hurts to see, for example, that my Dad's and Mother's Curtiss Flying Boat with a Hispano-Suiza engine is now sitting in the museum at Greenfield Village. But nowhere is it mentioned that Mother or Dad used to pilot that plane, that they donated it to the museum, that he or she worked for Henry Ford or was any part of his life.

As proof that this is the same one, Dad's registration is either riveted or screwed to the dash—and I have a picture of it taken at the museum.

I suddenly recall how, when Mother was going to take off from the water, if the day was too calm, a speedboat would have to run ahead and make waves so that the suction would be broken under the hull for the plane's takeoff. I believe it was usually Mother who used the flying boat.

Mother was, in fact, the first licensed woman pilot in the state of Michigan. When the first female pilots held a reunion in New York in 1930 on the occasion of the second annual New York Aviation Show, they organized themselves into the "Ninety-niners" and had a booth at the show, where they signed autographs.

On another occasion Mother was honored at a luncheon at the Book Cadillac Hotel in Detroit for being the first woman pilot in Michigan. Amelia Earhart flew in for the ceremony.

Mother was quite different from Mrs. Clara Ford. That was probably what so attracted Ford that he would spend several fortunes on her in lavish gifts—including horses, planes, homes, and land—and what kept them together in an intimate relationship that started when she was still in her teens and he was in his late forties.

Mrs. Ford was serene and quiet. Mother was volatile and dynamic.

Mrs. Ford liked to read or sew. Mother was a tomboy who

would rather hike with Ford or go horseback riding alone (he wouldn't ride with her).

Mrs. Ford was so gentle that her husband gave her the nickname Callie. Mother was such a tomboy that he gave her the nickname Billy, and Billy she became to Ray Dahlinger as well. Everyone else called her Mrs. D. To all the executives at the plant, to the executives' wives when they came to our parties, and even to the little children at the Village school, she was Mrs. D. Actually, Dad shortened her nickname to Bill, and that is what I remember his calling her. In letters that I have come across since Dad's death, however, I noticed that when I was just a little boy he sometimes addressed her as "Honey girl."

Mrs. Ford spent her time walking in the garden. Mother had mastered the Roman trick of riding while standing on two horses. She was the tristate women's harness racing champion.

Mrs. Ford was a miser. Mother threw money around riotously. Ford loved it. He was the same way.

And, quite probably out of their love and happiness together, I was born. I did not know at first that people suspected Henry Ford was my father. The town of Dearborn seemed to know. But I didn't. The fellows at the local bars seemed to know, and at the Dearborn Country Club, but I did not know. As a tiny tot I was taught to be very respectful to the elderly gentleman who spent all the time he could with me, and to call him sir and Mr. Ford.

I was "an open secret" to those who knew Ford and his family. But the amenities were kept in those days. And if, for example, Mrs. Ford wondered about my true identity and why Mr. Ford kept me around so much and wanted me to play with his grandchildren, she never let on.

But it's hard to believe that she did not eventually notice that I looked very much like a younger edition of her son, Edsel. I have a picture of myself and a picture of Edsel taken years apart when we were both about the same age, and the resemblance is uncanny.

Mrs. Ford would pat me on the head and have a servant get

me a cookie, but later she seemed moody, sometimes liking me, sometimes not. Sometimes liking Mother, sometimes not.

Although Henry Ford had a bit of a sense of humor himself, he leaned on Mother and me to amuse him, and on Father to tell him the rougher funny stories. One sample of Ford's sense of humor was the telephone numbers he gave out to the few trusted employees to whom he wanted to be directly connected. The number he dreamed up for Dad was Walnut 5.

Dad told him he wasn't sure he liked that number. "I don't want to be a nut."

Mr. Ford retorted, "A nut can't help being a nut; but don't worry—I like nuts." So the private line to our house remained Walnut 5.

Most of the time when people laughed at something Henry Ford said, he later complained that he didn't know what they were laughing about because he meant it seriously. For example, when he said history was a lot of bunk, he meant it.

Now and then Ford would display a fiendish little-boy sense of humor. Once he had a box of exploding cigars, and he had a little fun testing out the reactions of his friends. But he didn't like practical jokes played on him.

I suppose that somewhere in the back of my mind I always knew I was Henry Ford's illegitimate son. Why else was I getting this royal treatment? My relationship with him was certainly more personal than any he extended to other of his employees' children. I saw more of him than his own grand-children did.

Also, he took much more of a personal interest in every detail of my life and its direction than would be expected or usual, even from one who was in love with my mother. In fact he was forever trying to get me away from Mother for periods of time; he wanted me around all by myself. He wanted the two of us to do things in a buddy-buddy fashion.

I never really showed Mr. Ford the affection I think he hungered for. He wanted to be around me so much, and I could never, as a child, figure out why.

As I grew older, he was shy about using the word *love*, but I do have a telegram, sent to me when I was six, which uses the word:

MIAMI BEACH FLA   APR 9 1929

DEAR JOHN   HAPPY BIRTHDAY   MUCH LOVE   HENRY FORD

To show how much my mother cherished everything that came from Ford, I recently found this telegram stuffed into an old purse with many other reminders of him.

Any time the elderly gentleman who was Henry Ford tried to show affection, it was an emotion-charged moment that I would avoid. As a child, I just didn't know how to handle it.

I didn't do much better the night a date asked me pointblank, "Say, are you really the bastard son of Henry Ford?"

Almost automatically, I shouted back, "Hell, no!" and indicated that she could pass the word around.

Through the years I have discovered that the damnedest people have heard of my supposed illegitimacy and Ford connection. Mel Tormé asked my wife, Bette, about it. Jackie Leonard, the comedian, intimated it on the Mike Douglas show when talking about Act IV, the supper club I owned, at which he had appeared. My brother-in-law runs into the question now and then while playing golf. Of course he could always wear a T-shirt saying, "My brother-in-law is not the bastard son of Henry Ford."

Except, of course, the T-shirt might not be true, but it does point up the fact that it's more the people around me who have to bear the brunt of this thing. Most people are not as outspoken with me as the brash girl on that early date.

One time my wife Bette and I were at a party. Having been served, Bette looked around for a place to sit. A man offered her the seat next to him and lost no time in telling her how lucky she was to be at that party.

"Why so?" Bette asked.

"You see that man over there by the bar?" the man replied.

Bette looked and saw me standing some distance away at the bar. "Yes," she said.

"Well, *that man*," he paused impressively, "is the illegitimate son of Henry Ford." He stopped to see what effect his startling information had had.

Bette said, "Oh, really? I know him."

"No!" the man said, greatly impressed.

"Yes," she answered with a sly smile. "I sleep with him. He's my husband."

Years before that, when I was getting divorced, my first wife, who had heard rumors around town that I was the illegitimate son of Henry Ford, wanted to get a big settlement by proving my ancestry.

My mother was still in fairly good health at that point, and such a disclosure would have greatly distressed her. And Ray Dahlinger, the man I'd called Dad all through the years, was still alive. I pulled a typical Henry Ford bluff and said, "Great. If your lawyer can prove it, I'll split an empire with you." She believed my ploy, and I succeeded in throwing her off the trail.

I had been living with this knowledge for years, but I was not about to go public and drag the family through endless court proceedings. It would have been damn sensational.

However, even had I taken it to court and proven it beyond a shadow of a doubt, Mother still would have remained silent or denied it to the grave.

But here I must explain another reason, perhaps the most important of all, for writing this book. So much has been written about Ford—how great he was, and how he put America on wheels—that the public has lost sight of the eccentric flesh-and-blood man behind the cardboard poster.

Now that I am fifty-five, I believe I am the only person still around who knew Ford in the special intimate way that I did from the first day of my life. I know that as a child I spent much more time with him than his own grandchildren did. And he was in my home much more than he was in theirs.

If I do not tell what I know—what I remember of him, all the things that Mother said and Dad said and that I overheard, as well as what I have found in the vast accumulation of Mother and Dad's papers and memorabilia—who will?

Yes, if I don't tell, who will?

2
"The Other Woman"– My Mother

It seems strange to be talking about Mother as "the other woman" in someone's life, but that, I feel, is exactly what she was. It's the kind of thing that a son may know and observe, but the hard part is putting the proper title on it and calling it what it was.

I think Henry Ford really loved my mother—he certainly spent enough time with her and proved it in every way possible—and I think Mother loved him.

She certainly seemed to be obsessed with him and kept track of everything he was doing day by day in her diaries. She seems to have destroyed some of her diaries as she grew older and more discreet; even so, I found enough of the little books secreted around the house, painstakingly written by hand (partly in French), to get a good picture of their relationship.

The question naturally arises: Why Evangeline? With all the

young women who worked at the various Ford plants and all the women he met socially, why did the powerful tycoon of industry choose the little French girl?

Maybe it was just that Ford admired gutsiness. Evangeline Côté, the young woman who became my mother, had guts to spare. When her father became ill when she was sixteen, Evangeline went to work at the Ford Motor Company to support her whole family. She was the oldest child, the only girl; she had three young brothers to help raise. Her father was a professor, and in those days professors did not earn enough to put anything away. He was a French-Canadian who had emigrated to Michigan when he married my grandmother, Agatha Reheaume. She and Tyrone Power's mother were sisters.

Somehow, teaching herself, practicing far into the night at home, she became so efficient that in three years, at a mere nineteen, she rose to head of the stenographic department at the Highland Park plant.

Then, by chance, she got the break that put her where Henry Ford could notice her. One of Ford's favorites, C. Harold Wills, a gifted draftsman and engineer who had been with Ford since 1903, made Evangeline his personal secretary.

Now Ford could not help but see the striking young woman whenever he came to see Wills. She had a saucy tongue and flashing dark eyes and was a natural coquette. Wills was starting to get interested in Evangeline, too, but Ford snatched her away. Wills didn't have a chance.

Soon Ford was taking up much of her time, and Evangeline began working directly for the Boss as sort of a personal assistant, dividing her time between the two men.

It's important to realize the many differences between them—the age difference, for example. Ford was born in the third year of the Civil War, and Evangeline was born in 1893. There were thirty years between them.

Ford was a very rigid person, known to be hell on wheels if any member of his family or an employee strayed from the home fires. Evangeline was fun-loving and full of laughter in spite of her responsibilities, and she easily twisted men around her little finger. Even as a boy I could see that.

From what I have been able to piece together, when Ford found himself entangled with this vibrant young woman, he tried to save himself by throwing her at an eligible young man, hoping to marry her off. The man was Raymond C. Dahlinger, one of Henry Ford's trusted employees.

Later he would be one of the very loyal Ford men who would, as ordered, report to Henry Ford on what other employees were saying and doing. Before his marriage, however, Dad was basically a test driver.

From her diaries I know that Mother was desperate to get married and have a child—or, to be more accurate, she was desperate to have a child, and no matter how enlightened and modern one was in those days, one still had to get married first.

Of course there was no chance of her ever marrying Henry Ford; so Evangeline set her cap for Ray Dahlinger, and Henry Ford set Ray's cap for Evangeline. In no time Ray was writing beautiful love letters to her.

And so they were married. Mother was twenty-three; the date was February 20, 1917. What made it very dashing was that Dad had gone on the Peace Ship with Henry Ford to try to stop the war in Europe, and he was returning to his love and for the wedding a year later.

But the reality of marriage was not everything Evangeline had hoped for, particularly since she did not become pregnant. She was working very hard for Ford, and she was helping her husband advance his career as well—he had been made manager of all the Ford farms—but she felt unfulfilled. The years were moving along, and she still did not have a baby—1918, 1919, 1920, and on.

The marriage was a strained one, and increasingly Evangeline got her enjoyment and her deeper rewards from the companionship of Henry Ford. She became deeply immersed in anything the Boss wanted to do. In 1919 Henry Ford started the renovation of his birthplace, and she was largely in charge of that. In 1920 Edsel Ford started his house on Gaukler Pointe in Grosse Pointe, Michigan. Evangeline was in charge of many of the house's finer points and decorations.

In her diary for Wednesday, November 24, 1920, she states that she is lonesome and wishes she had a couple of children. She talks of the cold, of a furnace that was out at the large farmhouse Ford had provided for them, of a walk with Mr. Ford, a ride with the Boss. In her diary, Ford is usually referred to simply as the Boss.

The diary entries continue, always built around Ford and the Ford family—consulting with Mrs. Ford, buying Christmas presents for Mrs. Ford, walks with the Boss, rides with the Boss. Still no baby.

It is almost a relief to finally read that on April 9, 1923, John Côté Dahlinger was born to Evangeline C. Dahlinger and Raymond C. Dahlinger. The birth was at Henry Ford Hospital at 11:37 A.M. on a Monday. (Not that it matters, but he weighed 7 lb. 11 oz., or 3,500 g., and was 21½″ long.) The doctor was E. Plass.

Henry Ford shocked the hospital by arriving to take a look at the new baby. At age sixty he made no bones about the fact that this child was very special to him. The nurse in the maternity ward, Miss Lynch, was startled to meet Ford. She was even more startled when he ordered that she be brought to the Dahlinger house to look after me night and day. I was to have nothing but the best from day one.

On May 5, when I was not quite one month old, I received my first horse as a present from Henry Ford, a little Shetland colt that grew as I grew.

Miss Lynch was well paid for leaving the hospital to come live with me. I realize now it was a little amazing for a child to have a registered nurse around the house if he wasn't sick. I called her Nana; the grown-ups called her Lynchy. Lynchy was one of the family from the day I was born until I was twenty-four years old, when she had a stroke.

We would have her over for holidays like Thanksgiving. When Mother was out of town, Dad and Lynchy would take me places. She became a part of the family somewhat in the way that Ford was part of our family. Lynchy was extremely fond of Dad and emotionally dependent on him, but I don't know whether there was a deeper commitment or a romance. She spoke a lot about him in her diary.

Dad was not as large in my life as Mother, and I did not pay much attention to his activities. Mother had her room and Dad had his room, and I don't remember their sharing the same bedroom even when I was a child.

But with all the people around, I grew up in some kind of perpetual house party. Someone was coming and someone was going and people were having fun. One of my earliest memories is Mother's learning to fly and getting her pilot's license. I believe I must have been about four or five when she finally got her license. And I was four when she started carrying a concealed weapon—with Henry Ford's approval, of course, and that of the local authorities.

When I was four Mother helped Henry Ford start the school in Greenfield Village, which Ford was later to insist that I attend. In fact they moved the whole little school which he had attended as a child—lock, stock, and school desks. I have a picture of Mr. Ford, Dad and me in front of the Scotch Settlement School, as it was called.

In the school's early years, 1927 to maybe 1930, Mother helped pick the teachers and had the power to fire anybody who displeased her. She taught etiquette at the school and was considered the Emily Post of the area.

About the same time as Greenfield Village came into being, Henry Ford also started the construction of the Dearborn Country Club. I am still a member of that club, as are various Ford relatives and executives of the Ford Motor Company.

Though Mother and Dad did not seem to have an intimate relationship, they had a great working relationship in those early years. Together they worked on the renovation of some of the historical homes in Greenfield Village, and Mother did much of the research needed to refurbish them. She would travel many miles tracking down some object from Ford's childhood, bringing it back in triumph.

She went back and forth to New York on buying trips for the Village, purchasing antiques and arranging for reproductions. I still have letters from the owner of Kittenger Furniture—the company that made the ultimate in fine furniture—thanking Mr. Ford for the superb work that Mrs. Dahlinger had done, and remarking that in her tenacity in reconstructing history she was a tribute to Ford.

Ford enabled Mother to live in high style. She stayed at only the best places and was highly catered to. I have run across this letter from a top executive of New York's St. Moritz Hotel:

Cable Address: SANMORITZ

> St. Moritz on-the-Park
> Fifty Central Park South
> New York 19, N.Y.

March 19, 1953

Dear Mrs. Dahlinger:

Such a long period of time has elapsed since your last visit to the St. Moritz that we are wondering whether it is through any inadvertent fault of ours that you have not returned.

If this is so—we will appreciate your telling us just what the trouble was, so that we may remedy it and leave nothing in the way of your return. If it isn't so—and we hope it isn't—please accept this letter as an assurance of a hearty welcome should occasion bring you back to us again.

> Sincerely yours,
> St. Moritz on-the-Park
> (signed)

When Ford and his wife were at their winter homes in Georgia or Florida, Mother kept in touch with Ford through his secretary. I have many exchanges of letters between Ford's secretary, Frank Campsall, and my parents that show the humor that flowed between them, and also how quickly Mother responded to any note from him, knowing that it also came from Henry Ford.

Here is one of Mother's letters containing a take-off on the "Daily Dirt Digest." This was a little sheet which we schoolkids put out in the Village. At the time she sent these items, I was eleven. But before you read the first two, it is important to know that Lovett was the dance master, Simonds was the curator in charge of the Ford Museum under Dad, and Jehle was Thomas Edison's laboratory assistant.

*** Daily Dirt Digest ***

(Only what you'd hear if you were here anyway, and thought it might give you a laugh)

Item No. 1.

"It is reported that Mr. Benj. B. Lovett is opening the Greenfield High School in the Museum Bldg. Monday or Tuesday next. This is a little sooner than expected, we surmise, cause they didn't have time to order desks but had to make them."

Item No. 2.

"When the coast was rather clear the other day and there wasn't too many around, the Guides and Mr. Simonds of Greenfield Village had a 'Mutual Admiration Committee Meeting' at the Chapel. Different ones (guides) got up and said how fine this one did, and that one did, and the crowning one was 'what a wonderful man Mr. Simonds was, how fortunate they were to have him for their chief, how he had done a lot of research for the play and got things in it that no one else knew about, not even Mr. Jehle' (boy that wasn't any lie), and there sat Simonds all alone, way up front, with his coat open and his thumbs in the armholes of his vest, beaming like to burst. Nevertheless we still think they put on a good show."

Getting those Village gossip items out of the way, Mother went on to other things:

We have been sending milk, butter and cream, about every other day; let us know if there is too much or too little?

Glad to hear the Boss and Mrs. made the trip O.K. Hope the sunshine will do them both good and that Mrs. gets a good rest and is all well soon again. Don't let too many people bother her, Frank, eh? She tries to do too much for her own good. Jane Hicks sent a lot of telegrams and air mail letters about the Garden Club before anyone had a chance to make up their minds about things. Hope you stopped them—as things are now, the Garden Club is working on something altogether different. Don't bother Mrs. but did you by any chance get her approval on the paint samples. Wish you'd send them on as soon as possible if you did. Tell her everything is O.K. at the residence.

Called Mrs. Campsall and she said everything was fine and everyone was well. Your office looks a bit empty but they don't seem to be getting thin from lonesomeness—that's not talking for our office you know. But then, well, how have you been any-way? But then no fooling, it was so nice to hear from you, and know about everyone and everything. You know, the place is sorta lost with the folks gone, even though everyone is working like the dickens to get lots done for when they come back. You'll have to be taking time off to read this if we don't stop soon. Will write again, goodbye, and take care of yourself.

At this point, Mother must have checked at the plant to see if there was any other news and decided to add one more goodie, which was guaranteed to make Mr. Ford gnash his teeth. But she wrote it up innocently, tongue in cheek:

Report on "44" Job

Feb. 21, 1934.

Car was put on test track at Rouge with up-to-date brakes. After 50 stops clutch began to slip. Removed motor and found oil seal in clutch housing worn out allowing oil to get to clutch plates causing slip. Motor had had oil leak at transmission.

Installed a different motor and put on test track. Oil plug either fell out or was knocked off in testing causing motor to lose all oil and burn out bearings. Found clutch perfectly dry. Installed a new rebuilt motor with special oil seal in clutch housing. Car was put on test track and run about a day and front radius rod broke causing brake to lock and throw axle and steering rods out of alignment. Radius rod broke at front end rear axle. Radius rods not strong enough to stand heavy strain of brake test.

From the time I was born, Ford tried to see to my future. He could not give us stock in the company, because that would have caused all kinds of repercussions in the family and in the company. All Ford stock was at that time family-owned.

Instead, he tried to provide for my family with valuable gifts and property. When I was four, Mother acquired land and started building a summer home near Ford's own summer place. When completed, it had a main house, tennis house, carriage house, windmill guest house, beach house and bath house, and a large barn. It also had a private seaplane docking ramp for their personal plane.

Then Mr. Ford gave Mother and Dad a 300-acre farm in nearby Romeo. It had an old farmhouse, a new house, and several barns. The folks had a lake constructed for enjoyment and to water the 300 head of cattle they also received—one cow per acre.

Still, that was only the warm-up. Mother really went overboard in her winter (or year-round) house, a Tudor manor. The construction was started in 1930, when I was seven. It took nine years to build, using the best of everything that Ford could provide. Mother wanted to live in a house similar to Mrs. Ford's, only more to her taste. I suppose it was a matter of vanity.

When the Fords were ready to build Fairlane—I still have stationery from the days it was spelled Fair Lane—they called in Frank Lloyd Wright to get his thinking about design. He made plans for a marvelous contemporary structure that would keep step with progress.

Ford was horrified at the new concept of architecture, and retreated into the most conservative building he could find. It was impressive, yes, but certainly not functional. Mother would laugh and say Ford's house got the highest marks—among the ugly ducklings.

Mother wanted a swan of a house, something that nestled in the ground and yet soared above it; something that had the charm of beautiful stone, rich woods, and picturesque balconies.

I have the deed from Henry Ford to my parents for the tract of land on which the house sits, giving them approximately 150 acres "for and in consideration of the sum of one dollar ($1)." Not a bad buy.

Somehow Ford got his wife to sign the deed, which was necessary for its legality. Mrs. Ford was a Victorian-type woman who never crossed her husband, even when she suffered deeply—as she did when she thought Henry was being overly harsh with their son, Edsel.

Even though Henry Ford put a third of the Ford stock in his wife's name, she did not try in any way to assert herself or do anything but his bidding. Probably Mother had a lot more influence on the inner workings of the company. She surely gave her thinking freely to Ford, and they'd have heated conversations on how things should be done, with Mother suggesting that maybe this or that should be tried.

Mother had a good sense of land potential, and she would go scouting for land for the Ford farms. Then Dad and Mr. Ford would go out and check the land; if they agreed with her appraisal, Ford would purchase it.

Getting back to Mother's dream house, the whole place was referred to—and still is—as the Dahlinger estate. The estate eventually included a gate barn, which housed a twenty-four-hour guard; a Kentucky show barn (a barn with a balcony to look down on the horses); a working barn; a single-story stall barn with corrals; a blacksmith's shop; a lake with skating house (Ford and Mother loved to skate together); a half-mile race track with a large heated starter house; a quarter-mile cinder track; a six-car garage; a beautiful middle-sized house dubbed "the carpenters' shanty," which was anything but a shanty for workmen to use; a greenhouse with servants' quarters which were nice enough to later be made into an apartment for me as a young man; a boat house; a farmhouse with three garages (one for Dad, one for Mother, one for me); and, last but not least, the main house.

Before I tell you about the main house that Ford built for us, I'd better let you know that Mother was a fireplace freak, as the young would label her today. The main house has nine fireplaces, one more fireplace than it has bathrooms. It also has a four-car garage with a mechanic's hoist so that a Ford expert could come and make repairs on the spot.

There are comfortable servants' quarters, and a flower room, where flowers could be arranged for the other rooms without messing up those rooms. There is a refrigerated fur-storage vault. There was a room for an indoor pool, which, however, could never be installed, because the Rouge River would overflow and cause drainage back-up.

There is even a secret staircase. It is hard to know whether even Dad knew that this secret entrance to Mother's dressing room was being installed. This is indeed the major secret of the house. A person could go into a certain small room downstairs and disappear into the secret staircase that led up to Mother's suite. One could also leave the same way without being observed.

I was the first one to move into the house, and for a few months I lived there all alone except for the servants.

The situation between Mother and Dad had deteriorated. There was a growing amount of jealousy because of all that Ford was doing for Mother. Not that Dad didn't benefit too, or that Ford didn't try to do nice things for him, because he did. But Mother had become a little high-handed—or, as Dad put it, "she had delusions of grandeur"—and was trying to manage Dad's life and tell him what to do to "better himself."

Dad was drinking more and more. He said he was perfectly happy living in the old farmhouse and didn't want to live in a "goddamn castle." Evidently Mother did. The house was her magnificent obsession. She kept changing and revising the house plans.

Sometimes a wall was torn down and moved a foot in one or the other direction. Once, when she changed her mind, all the furnace ducts had to be moved to conform with her revised wishes, and the furnace men had to be called back.

Mother had at her disposal the Ford craftsmen, many of whom had been brought from Europe to work at Greenfield Village—including woodcarvers and ironsmiths. She would annoy Dad greatly by speaking French to some of these men, which Dad could not understand; and she would always speak French to our gardener, who was also a horticulturist and a graduate of a college in Belgium.

When I was sixteen or seventeen and the house had been finished for months, their situation had reached the point where neither Mother nor Dad would take the first step to move into the new house. Poor Mr. Ford didn't know what to do. He tried to get Dad to tell him what was bothering him. Dad said he was afraid that if he moved into this big house, Mother's parents were going to move in with them. It was as good an excuse as any.

But Henry Ford wouldn't let him get away with it. He had a brilliant idea. Equal treatment. If Mother's parents were to live with us, he would build a summer house for Dad's mother. It was called Belleville, after the town in Michigan where he chose to build it. Dad built a complex of buildings for his mother that was really something—200 acres with an Anne Hathaway–type lake house and various outbuildings, including a boat house with a tunnel to the lake house in case of rain.

It was really very ironic, since Dad's mother didn't even want the house because it took her away from her cronies at Dearborn, away from her son, and thirty miles from where she'd lived.

But this just goes to show the character of Henry Ford. Once he made up his mind he was going to do something "nice" for someone, he viewed the quaint notion that the person didn't want it done as just some annoyance that he had to contend with. Henry Ford did what he thought best in spite of details like that.

If I have learned anything from Henry Ford, it is independence. I let Mother and Dad stay in the old house and fight it out, and I packed up and moved into the new house alone. After all, I felt that, in the final analysis, Ford had meant the house for me.

The details of the house were indeed magnificent. In my suite, there was not a single knob or drawer pull. All dresser drawers were built in and pulled out silently and magically. Pewabic tiles in the various bathrooms were exotic and unusual. I had my own fireplace, of course. The maid kept my clothes in my large closet, sorted and hung in perfect order according to the color of the suits, the material, and the purpose, casual or dress. There were also, naturally, the proper clothes for every sport: tennis, car racing, riding, sailing, soccer, golf, lacrosse, and hiking and camping.

Fortunately, after I had lived in the house awhile, Dad and Mother followed me, and things were again serene on the surface. They seemed busy and happy in their separate pursuits. They slept at opposite ends of the house, respecting each other's privacy.

As for my quarters, I was able to tease Mother about having made one of the passageways to my suite so narrow I had to go through sideways. She replied, "This way I know you'll never get fat."

I never did gain weight and have always been slim and wiry, much the way Henry Ford and Edsel were.

Mother dressed ahead of her time. She was the first woman I knew who wore pants suits, and she looked good in them. She was only 5′1″ and very slim, but amply curved.

She was what we would call today a "liberated" woman, having her own career and making her own decisions. Once she made her mind up on anything, she persevered until she got what she was after.

Yet I would say that Mother was one of the most feminine females I have ever encountered. She was so adept at handling people—me, Ford, Dad, all the people she dealt with in reconstructing historic houses for Ford and his pet Greenfield Village—that we all eventually found ourselves going her way.

Of course I don't know how much she influenced Ford in big things. I only know she did influence him in many little things.

Mother was the person Ford counted on most to decorate the interiors of the historic houses he bought and transplanted to Greenfield. She decided frequently—or helped to make up Henry Ford's mind—on whether a certain building should be bought for the Village. I don't know how many homes or other buildings were not transplanted because she did not like them or felt they were unworthy in one way or another.

As I've said, Mother was the first woman in the state of Michigan to receive a pilot's license. Ford did not approve of her flying, but there was nothing he could do about it. She was headstrong and independent, which was part of her charm for him. But he did fuss and fume and tell her that the airplane was like a horse—no human could really control it. He refused to fly with her.

There was only one person who could get Ford into a plane—even though the Ford Motor Company made planes and had its own airport—and that was Charles Lindbergh. Ford said he figured the man who had flown a plane in darkness above the ocean knew what he was doing by daylight, and he took his first and only plane ride with him. It was in the *Spirit of St. Louis*, and Ford had to be practically jackknifed in, it was so small inside.

Later, when Lindbergh couldn't get a job during World War II, he went to work at the bomber plant at Willow Run as a quality-control man. He would come over to Dearborn to have lunch with Ford. At this point, I didn't see much of Mr. Ford because I was in the service.

Henry Ford in the early days had another famous pilot, Harry Brooks, on his payroll. Brooks was a hell of a pilot, but he made one fatal mistake off the Florida coast.

Only three people ever flew the Ford Flivver—Harry Brooks, Charles Lindbergh and me. After Brooksie died in the plane, it was rebuilt and during the war was kept at Ford Airport. I wanted to fly it, so I asked Lindbergh. "It's all right with me if you really want to, but I wouldn't get near the thing. I think you had better ask Mr. Ford."

So I trotted over to Fairlane and asked the Boss. "If it's all right with your Mother and Dad, it's all right with me."

So I trotted off home and asked Dad. "Sure, you're a good enough pilot. Just remember it doesn't have brakes."

I was a naval aviator and instructor by that time, and it was a challenge. So I took it up, and not only didn't it sound too good; it didn't run very well, either. I was up five minutes and never left the airport area, so that if I had had to, I could have landed in a hurry.

As I look back, it wasn't as much fun as flying the Mooney-Mite. But now I had flown the famous Flivver, which had set the world's distance record—on one tank of fuel in a light plane—in 1928.

The full story of how Harry Brooks met his death is not well known. He had been part of the little group that worked in secret to produce a small single-seat plane called the Ford Flivver. It was supposed to be the "Model T of the air," which would make it possible to put a plane in every garage.

Dad was one of the group in on building the plane, along with two test pilots, Harry Russell and Shorty Schroeder. An engineer named Hicks had designed the two-cylinder engine.

Lindbergh came and flew it; he had to take his shoes off to fly it, because the plane had been built for an average-size man.

The plane was a prototype. Two were built. Brooksie, as they called Harry Brooks, was the test pilot for the project. The plane had a fatal flaw—it was a single seater.

As someone asked Ford, "How are you going to teach someone to fly? Where would he sit?" No record exists of Ford's answer.

Anyway, Brooksie did use the plane to set time-distance records for a single-engine aircraft.

Now to tell how he was killed. He had landed at an airport on the Florida coast and the wind was blowing sand over his plane. Brooksie was afraid of getting sand in the gas tank. He inserted a toothpick in the gas cap's breather vent. Unfortunately, when he took off the next day he forgot to remove the toothpick, and the fuel line ran dry. The engine quit and the plane landed in the ocean off the Florida coast. Brooksie was seen on the wing in the water before the plane sank.

When the wreckage was recovered several days later, the toothpick was still in the gas cap. They never found his body.

There was a story that someone said he'd caught a shark with Harry Brooks's ring in its stomach. The ring was sent to Dearborn, and Mother said it was not his ring. But the legend remained.

After Brooksie's crash, Henry Ford forbade Mother and Dad to fly. Since at the time I was still pretty young, he didn't include me in his dictum.

He wasn't to know until much later that I had already been flying regularly with the pilot who ran an independent flying service at the Ford Airport. His name was Captain Johns, though I'm not quite sure what he was captain of. Since Dad ran the airport as part of the Ford farms, Captain Johns was always eager to give me a ride, maybe figuring it would help insure his lease.

He didn't have a copilot, and I would sit in the cockpit on pillows; I must have been about nine, but I still couldn't reach the rudder bars. When I was sixteen or seventeen I received my license, but in truth I had been flying for years. When Mr. Ford heard that I had my license, he frowned and said, "Remember Harry Brooks."

Did Ford have an eye for the ladies? Yes, he did. The maids at the Ford mansion were always threatening to tell Mrs. Ford that the Boss had pinched them or grabbed them and squeezed them intimately. Once Mother intercepted a note that a maid had planned to give to Mrs. Ford. In fact, whenever she could, Mother would screen Mrs. Ford's mail and spare her the hurt of letters like this one, from a former maid:

Dear Mrs. Ford

The first thing I went on the Ford Estate Mrs. A. put that filth in my mind. She told me I was too *dumb* I didn't know how to get money. Mrs. Ford I may look dumb but I am no fool.

She told me when Mr. Ford was *near me* in the kitchen I should *kiss* him and get something out of him.

I never got a penny in a dishonest way, so I hope to starve to death before I earn the money in a way that *Mrs. A.* does.

(signed)

The letter raved on for several pages about wild goings-on in the servants' quarters between the butlers and the maids. Part of it was a plea for money; there is some indication that Mother took care of it and sent her some money to tide her over, especially since she claimed to have done some extra service for the family. It is doubtful that Henry Ford ever knew about the letters—there were several.

My own thinking is that Ford at seventy was simply trying to show that he was still as vigorous and virile as men half his age. I think that at this stage he was content in his relationship with Mother and was not hunting for more involvements.

Still, to be a Ford meant one false move and he *was* involved. Once, one woman servant caught another one in the garden with Mr. Ford, who was making advances to her. A serious situation was shaping up, and Mother, in cahoots with one of the trusted men around Ford, helped arrange for her to decide that she wanted to take a job elsewhere; I think a little money helped make up her mind.

Mrs. Ford wondered what had gotten into her servant, who had always seemed so contented; I trust she never found out. As I recall, the servant left behind was still a threat to the tranquility of Fairlane, so she, too, was encouraged to leave for parts unknown, with the help of a little bribe. Now the secret of Ford's naughty behavior was safe—for a while. In fact, Mother probably never let on that she knew what had happened.

Mother was not particularly superstitious, but there was one thing she would not do. She would say, "Don't ever sign anything on Friday." I don't know why; I have never seen her so adamant about anything of a superstitious nature.

Mother felt, with some kind of female intuition, that Edsel Ford was a child of tragedy. It is ironic that even after his death, the very car named for him—the Edsel—also became a tragedy for the Ford Motor Company, even though it has now become a collector's item.

Mother had a soft spot for Edsel, whom she considered very handsome, and maybe this was one of the reasons why Ford was so hard on his son.

Ford was really a very jealous man. Mother thought it was because his own mother had died at a very early age. He was so hungry to have someone's affection that when he knew someone was fond of him, he wanted to possess that person totally.

He wanted to possess his son Edsel totally. He possessed Mother and Dad totally. And he tried to possess me totally—but I squirmed away.

I remember one time Mother was very worried about something she had learned Mr. Ford was going to do to embarrass his son, and she phoned Edsel in New York to alert him so that he could think of some way to avoid the situation. But he had already started on his way back to Dearborn, and there was nothing she could do.

Dad would tell her of the Boss's tricks, thinking they were funny, and of course not knowing that she didn't think they were funny at all; she was just pumping him so that she could warn Edsel. I remember once Ford had a good idea where such a leak had come from; he was at our house looking very grim. I was surprised to see Mother looking very indignant too.

She was not afraid of him, and I can still hear her giving Mr. Ford a piece of her mind. "You can't do this. It just isn't nice. How can he ever be independent with you stepping on him?"

It was amazing to me that Mother could get away with telling Ford what she thought, whereas Dad was very subservient and usually agreed with anything Ford said.

But Ford grumbled a little bit longer, saying, "Well, I never thought you'd be the one to go piddling in his ear." That was one of Ford's favorite expressions. If you were telling something you shouldn't, you were piddling in someone's ear.

That was his *polite* way of putting it. Around men, his language could be very rough. More than once I heard him tell someone that "So-and-so is a goddamned son of a bitch and I want him out of here."

As Ford grew older and weaker, Evangeline Dahlinger's powers waned too. I would say that her last hurrah concerned the U.S.S. *Dearborn*. Ford sent her to christen the ship.

A year later, at the commissioning, celebrities and movie stars came to participate in the wartime ceremony, and she was the queen of the show. I still have a picture of her with Victor Mature, with an inscription attesting to her power at the time.

I recently talked with one of the old-timers—who naturally did not know I was working on this book—and he volunteered that in her day my mother had more power at Ford Motor Company than the president of most companies had.

I am sure it is safe to say that while Edsel was president she must have had as much power as he did—at least with the real head of the company, Henry Ford.

3
Growing Up Ford

I had no notion that my life was anything other than aver-age—at least when I was young.

Didn't every young child have a bodyguard? Didn't every young child have a nanny? The abundance of servants who were around the estate, the special privileges, places, and people that made up my life were, to me, ordinary occurrences of everyday living.

Didn't every young child have an operating gas-powered car at the age of five? During the Great Depression my family's gravest concern was coping with the problems of buying, ex-panding, and developing—was this piece of land better than that one?

When school time came, I went to the Scotch Settlement School in Greenfield Village. I sat at the same desk he had used as a child, and we used the same McGuffey readers that he had.

Ford was very particular about making sure that I was as-signed to his old seat.

I did not know that it was openly rumored that I was the "bastard son" of Henry Ford. People did not talk about it in my hearing. But evidently plenty of talking did go on. And it was not lost on the town that I was frequently in the company of the great man.

When I was nine or ten, a kid in school called me a bastard and yelled, "That is not your real father. Mr. D. is not your real father!"

I fought him and he won. I hardly knew what I was fighting about, except that I knew it was meant as an insult. He kept taunting me, and about twice a week I would have to fight him.

He always won. I might have had an occasional draw, but I was never able to defend my honor properly—or, rather, Mr. D.'s honor. This fellow was the first one to call me a bastard to my face and say that Ray Dahlinger was not my real father. At the time, I just thought he was being a nasty kid for no reason at all, and that he wanted to pick a fight.

But even at that stage, the repetition of the accusation made an imprint on my mind, and I finally asked my mother what he had meant, and what the word *bastard* meant. She said it was just a bad word and he was just a mean kid and to pay no attention, which was a little hard to do when it was my face that was getting battered.

Then came that early date, when I got it right between the eyes: "Say, are you really the bastard son of Henry Ford?"

Again I confronted Mother.

Dad and I knew Mother very well. If she didn't want to admit something, she'd say, "I don't want to talk about it."

Like, "Mother, did *you* put the dent in your car? Where did it happen?"

"I don't want to talk about it."

Or, when I was eight, "Mother, are you going away this weekend again? You promised you wouldn't."

"I don't want to talk about it."

That closed the subject, and you weren't supposed to inquire what was so important that it took her away from you. If she decided on her own to tell you, she would.

So now I said, "Mother, is it true that Henry Ford is my father?" hoping she would laugh and say, "How ridiculous!" But she didn't, and I didn't like the look on her face as she tried to sound casual: "Oh, you finally heard about that. Who were you talking to?"

I said, "You don't know her. Is it true?"

She said, "I don't want to talk about it."

My heart sank. She didn't have to say any more. I knew that was it, and that further conversation was unnecessary.

This is a partial list of the gifts Henry Ford gave me when I was just a little boy:

A cradle and the baby bed Ford had used as a baby
A rocking horse
A miniature gardening wagon and tools
A small horse-drawn sleigh
An electric buckboard car
A scaled-down horse-drawn buckboard
A red bike
A small-scale motorized roadster (at age five)
Snowball (my trick horse), which had come from Ringling
  Brothers circus
A midget race car (at age fourteen)
A Swiss clock—a man whistles (considered a mechanical oddity)
A small tractor
A pony

After I got into my teens and beyond, I received assorted horses and assorted cars. I still have pictures of many of these, and some of the cars may be seen in Greenfield Village Museum—though not identified as donated by my family.

I remember the Ford grandchildren as they used to be when I would be sent over to play with them at their grandmother's house, Fairlane. Josephine was the closest to me in age. But she was a girl, and it was a chore to be expected to play with her. We called her Dody.

Billy was the next closest, a couple of years younger. Benson was three years older than I was and Henry six years older. I did not consider any of them much fun to play with. The trouble was that they wouldn't play—they weren't athletic.

To my lean eye, Henry and Benson were a couple of fatties. Mother said that it wasn't a nice thing to say and that they were only a little chubby. The point was they weren't running-and-screaming kids, like I was; they were sit-and-argue kids: "No I'm not." "Yes you are." "You took my ball." "No I didn't." "Get your own ball."

Henry Ford wanted us to play together. It was his idea, not mine. In my mind his grandchildren were spoiled, nasty little kids who wanted their own way. Actually, I was spoiled in my own way—and especially spoiled by their grandfather. But spoiled as I was, at least I did not ruin their toys the way they ruined mine.

Dody, as a little girl, was dark-haired and very pretty. She was relatively quiet, but once she got an idea for mischief, she could be a little devil.

Once she got hold of some of Mrs. Ford's books and drew on them and tore out some of the pages. I was sure that when it was discovered, I would be blamed. So I immediately went in and tattled on her to Mrs. Ford, so there could be no mistake about who had committed this desecration.

My concern was to protect myself, of course, but beyond that I was highly indignant that Dody did not have respect for books, which were highly regarded in our house.

I don't recall if her grandmother disciplined her, but she must have, because Dody did not appreciate me after that.

The older boys—Benson, who had some kind of eye problem, and Henry—seemed to do everything possible to wreck my cars without getting punished for it. They would ride them around and "accidentally" bump into everything possible, leaving them scratched and dented.

I don't recall which of them got into my Red Bug and drove it into the pond near the engineering building.

Cleverly, they didn't bring their own toys and cars for me to ruin in turn. Dody had one governess and Bill had another. I think Bill was the best natured of the lot, and though he was younger and smaller, I chose to play with him alone, whenever I could get away from the others. Perhaps I liked the fact that he *was* smaller and I could intimidate him. We played the games *I* chose.

Always athletically inclined, I won top honors in tennis and swimming. Now and then I run into my old swimming coach at the Dearborn Country Club and we reminisce. He recalls that he always thought I would be his Olympic diver. I was always a pretty good diver and swimmer, but I did not give it total attention. I participated in all the sports at school that I could.

Mr. Ford didn't believe in tackle football, so we had to play touch football. When I went away to Deerfield, I played football and lacrosse, a rugged game. And I was on the varsity swim team at Deerfield. I was junior high school champion in tennis at Greenfield Village.

I don't recall that Mrs. Edsel Ford—Eleanor—came with the kids when they were visiting their grandmother and playing with me. I just don't remember her being there on those occasions. The kids would come out with a driver from Grosse Pointe to Dearborn, about an hour away.

Mr. Ford would have someone phone for me. A car would come over or my own driver would take me. I was glad it wasn't too often.

I have several photographs of me playing with the Ford grandchildren, and I must say that in none of them are any of us laughing or looking particularly happy or excited. Boredom and doing our duty would be more like it. In one picture Dody Ford is having a ride in my miniature sleigh drawn by my pony. Since it was my horse and my sleigh, I held the lines; I don't think Dody was happy about it.

In another photo, Dody had finally gotten hold of the reins. This time we are in my wagon drawn by my trusty pony. It's winter, and we are all warmly dressed. Dody is alone in the driver's seat, and Billy and I are in the back—but I'm standing up, to make it clear who the rig belongs to. All told, I don't think they enjoyed the visits any more than I did.

In April of 1929, when Mrs. Ford asked Dad to build a playhouse in a tree for her grandchildren and me, the house contained nothing but the best: Coleman lanterns, hardwood pegged floor, screened windows, stairway up, front door screen, stained walls. One girl, Dody Ford, was allowed in, though I don't remember her using it much.

On my fifth birthday I was given a party. I had received presents from my parents and Lynchy and the maids and everyone else when Mr. Ford came by.

I was too polite to ask, but I felt a little surge of excitement as I wondered what his present would be. However, he merely said, "Happy birthday, John," and went to talk to Mother. I was a little aggrieved that my personal Santa Claus had come up empty-handed—and on my birthday, yet. The birthday cake was still to be cut; the maid, busy with the cake, sent me and my playmates outside to play.

Mr. Ford came out of the house, said good-by, and again wished me a happy birthday without giving me anything. I was on the verge of asking him about it, but I controlled myself.

When I got back into the house and headed for the birthday cake, I saw a car key at my plate. It belonged to a gas-powered car, hardly the thing you would bring inside the house. He had left my present on the half-mile harness horse track.

I remember that when Mother started to look around for property she fell in love with a certain parcel of land up north. Henry Ford came by to see it. It was near his own summer place. He said, "Billy, I want you to buy this for John." Then he hurried off, because he was on his way to Harbor Beach.

There always were guards around our estate, and I had my own bodyguard, at Mr. Ford's order.

There was quite a cast of characters around the farm. I remember Red John, who worked as handyman and was in charge of the hen houses. He had the kind of temper his name suggests. We kids would do anything to see him explode.

A friend and I would go in one door and scoop up all the eggs, then hightail it out onto the roof and wait for him to come looking for us. We would then pepper him with the eggs. We scored extra points if we mashed one into his red hair.

He was cutting the lawn once when I hit him on the fanny with a board. He took me in by the scruff of the neck; either he or my mother paddled me. I never did it again. It was unfortunate for me that Mother had been watching.

Then there was Pickem-up-shit Nick. I was talking with a friend about how run-down the Village looked now, compared to the days Dad had charge of it. When the horses would leave their droppings in the old days, they were immediately picked up by a man called Pickem-up-shit Nick. He was stocky, with a big black mustache and a very heavy accent.

You could hardly understand old Nick. One day he was found crying on the curb, and Mr. D. asked why he was crying. He said, "The horse, he shit seven days a week and Nick only work six." So Dad let him work seven days a week and made him a happy man. Nick never would have made it on a four-day work week.

My early memories of Ford are at the old farmhouse we lived in, which was beautifully furnished and which Ford had given us. Sometimes Ford would sit in the living room, but he seemed to particularly like the homey feeling of sitting in a kitchen. I guess it reminded him of his own childhood.

Whenever we sat around talking with Mr. Ford, the main topics of conversation were cars, the Village, his properties, our properties, problems at work, politics, and what he wanted me to do, think and achieve. He liked Herbert Hoover and hated Franklin Roosevelt with a passion. He would get very heated against Roosevelt, and at an early age I knew that Roosevelt was a dirty word.

I grew up around maids, chauffeurs, bodyguards, gardeners, a whole entourage of servants. Someone was always looking out for me, and yet I didn't feel that they infringed on my life. They were part of my life.

Special things were done for me. Maids would slip me a piece of cake. They knew that if I said nice things about them, Ford might give them a raise or some money.

As I look back, I was a little devil and a bratty kid. I always knew my place around adults, but I was always pushing to the limit with the kids. I always ran around with older kids. But, all in all, I was like most children. I remember whining because I had to go to bed at eight o'clock when other children had later hours.

I loved to wear cowboy boots. I was always riding horses or driving sulkies. The Shetland pony Mr. Ford gave me enjoyed a long life, dying in 1960. When I was about six or seven I remember feeding it a sugar cube the way you are supposed to, with flat palm, and the devil bit me. Took off some skin from my fingers. I hauled off and punched him one in the nose. He was a bratty horse like I was a bratty kid. We were some terrible team, always trying to get ahead of each other. Ford hated all animals, so it did no good to tell him about it. He said, "Humph. He's just a dumb horse, and anyone who plays with a horse had better be a little smarter."

I would have been insulted if one of my playmates, like the Ford grandchildren, had said such a thing. But since it was just Mr. Ford, I considered the source and let it go at that. Besides, Mother was always telling me to be polite to him, so I knew there would be the devil to pay if I got too sassy.

I knew how to tell time before I went to school, and in recognition of the fact Mr. Ford gave me my first watch. I wish I had it today, because it was engraved. I carelessly left it somewhere.

When I was seven or eight years old I was a good shot with a .22. Everybody taught me—Mother, Mr. Ford, and Dad. Mother was a hell of a shot. Anything Dad could do, she had to do better.

She soloed in a plane before he got his pilot's license. She shot better and rode better; she drove a sulky with a certain horse a half-second better than its trainer. She had hands that seemed naturally responsive to the vibes of the horse through the reins.

Every now and then she would purposely drive slower. "I have to let the men win sometimes or they'd be mad at me." She could beat Dad at tennis. The only thing she wouldn't do was ride a motorcycle. Dad had been hurt several times, and she learned her lesson from that.

I remember that Ford was always around until the time I went to school. Like Dad and Mother and the men who worked on the farm, he was just there. I remember that he had gray hair and that he was taller than Dad.

He wasn't extra special. I didn't hold him in any awe. The fact that he had invented a car didn't mean that much to me. I grew up around that car, and we had lots of them. Mother and Dad worked for him—that was all. There wasn't anything special in knowing him or in playing with his grandchildren.

Henry, Benson, Josephine and Billy were just like the rest of the kids I played with, except they seemed more worldly wise and didn't live on the farm. I knew Ford hated the place where they lived—Grosse Pointe—and I thought it must be a very wicked place.

When I was a child, Ford frequently rode his bicycle over from Fairlane. As we both grew older, his driver would deposit him in our lane and wait as long as necessary for him to come out. I recall that two drivers shared round-the-clock duty because Ford did not respect the clock.

If Ford stopped by in the daytime and I was digging in the mud, he would get right down on the ground with me, take one of my shovels and have a go at the digging too. If Dad came out of the house, he would call out and say, "Hello there, Ray. Is Billy home?"

Then he'd go in to see Mother, and they'd go cycling together. Dad would go driving off in his car. He accepted it. It was our way of life.

The dominant impression of my childhood was the hustle and bustle of my life revolving around Henry Ford. Something was always going on. Mother was being sent here or there by Ford. There was a message for her to be ready, and Mr. Ford's driver would pick her up. There was a message for Mother to pack a bag and take a train to New York or wherever.

When I was little it was always fun to walk with Mr. D. and Mr. Ford. I remember Mr. Ford would pick apples and other fruit off the trees and eat them. And as he munched he would say to Dad, "Do this and do that." "Tear that down." "Build that." "Send men here to take care of it." It was all done so matter-of-factly. I'm afraid he taught me at an early age how to give orders, too.

Ford liked going for sleigh rides wrapped in a buffalo robe. I remember cuddling down in that robe next to him.

The first time I was away from Mother and Dad was when I was, I believe, fifteen or eighteen months old. Lynchy took me to Port Austin with several of her nurse friends from Ford Hospital to stay at a cottage that Mother found.

They stayed for a month. During that time, Henry Ford wired to say hello to the baby, and later he stopped by to see how I was getting along. He had gone out of his way from Harbor Beach to see me. The nurses were all very flattered and in a twitter over the visit.

I was there again a second year. This time the big adventure was that I climbed a ladder and got on the roof and the nurses didn't know I had climbed it. When Lynchy saw me she climbed halfway up and asked me to come and help her down because she was stuck. It became a family story that I said, "You got up here, you can get down."

When I was six, on vacation at Grand Pré, I again felt adventurous. I had a few pennies in my pocket, and I decided to walk the mile into town to get some candy.

They discovered me missing and hit the panic button. They thought I had fallen into the ravine, which at that time was a fast-flowing stream.

Everyone was running around, looking in the ravine and in the lake and in the woods, and finally they found me. I was walking down the beach carrying a dead fish in one hand and holding a lollipop in my mouth. The local constabulary was already organizing a search party.

Mr. Ford was forever sending me telegrams—even before I could read. Here is one he sent me when I was three years old and he was on vacation near Port Austin.

RADIOGRAM

JULY 27 1926

MASTER JOHN DAHLINGER CARE MISS LYNCH DEARBORN

1045 AM TUESDAY WE ARE NOW PASSING POINT AUX BARQUE WE ARE
SENDING YOU GREETINGS FROM SIALIA

HENRY FORD

1123AM

I learned even as a small child that wherever I was, Mr. Ford was sure to show up.

He would find me, come upon me casually and sit down beside me, starting a casual conversation and imparting his philosophy or knowledge about life as he poked a stick at the ground. He seemed bent on telling me how to live, how to think, how to grow up to be part of his empire.

In whatever Mother planned to do, she automatically included Henry Ford or considered his wishes. Only once did I dare to suggest that we not take Mr. Ford with us. "Let's you and me go," I said.

I was just a little tyke, but I remember that Mother looked down at me in a way that I had never seen before. "Don't ever let me hear you say that again, John. Mr. Ford loves you very much, much more than I can express. And someday he wants you to help him run his whole company. Can you understand that?"

I really couldn't; it was a little confusing. Why would this old man love me? "Does he love me like Nana?" Now that was real love.

"Oh, much more than Nana."

"Does he love me like you do?"

"Yes, that's the way he loves you."

I wandered off to think that over. Now that was real, *real* love. Mother's whole life centered on me. When she wasn't with Ford or talking about Ford, she was with me or talking about me. When I would come upon her talking with Dad, John and the Boss seemed to be their favorite subjects.

Yes, Mother loved me, all right, but why this old man would care so much about me, I hadn't the foggiest notion.

Little by little I grew quite fond of the elderly gentleman. I would be sitting on a step, and he would show up somehow and sit beside me and pat my knee or the top of my head and say, "How's my little friend?" or "How's my favorite boy?"

I think that because I knew that somehow I mattered to him very much, I was determined to stay a bit aloof, to be my own man. Something in me was drawn to him, but I fought it.

It seems that everyone zeroed in on me when I was a baby. Even Lynchy was keeping a diary on my first two years. I found the diary mixed in with some of my mother's. One entry in Lynchy's diary ran:

February 9, 1924

> 20 lb., nine ounces, 10 mos. old today. Babe is very healthy and happy. Baby looks like a combination Socrates, Shakespeare, Beethoven and Michaelangelo. He is truly a genius.

Although she misspelled the artist's name, I certainly cannot complain about what she said. In fact I would blush to quote her, except that it shows to what extremes people were going to praise the baby in whom Henry Ford was showing so much interest.

Sometimes Ford would sit and tell me about his own childhood. A story that impressed me quite a bit at the time, and even more later, concerned his hilarious experiment with the water wheel as a source of power.

44

When he was about twelve or so, he got his classmates at the little school he attended—Miller School—interested in water power, and they dammed up the large local ditch near the school to provide the power for turning the wheel. Unfortunately, the damming of the waters flooded the farm next to the school, and the angry farmer took action. He demolished their water wheel.

No wonder Ford's handwriting was so terrible. He had time at school for everything but schoolwork. Another of his great experiments at school was to provide turbine power from steam. He set up a boiler and got the temperature of the water high enough to turn the turbine.

Unfortunately, the boiler blew up, and part of Miller School went with it. Foiled again!

I remember he told how he used to fix neighbors' watches and clocks in his room after school to earn a little pin money. There was no central heating, no fireplace or stove in his room. He kept his feet warm by turning a lantern on high and placing it on the floor in front of his feet. The light for the close work was provided by a kerosene lamp on his little desk.

If memory serves, I posed as young Ford for the artist who was painting that particular scene from Ford's childhood—at Ford's request, of course.

I can't remember a day of my childhood when I didn't hear the name Henry Ford. Mother and he were that close.

Mother and Mr. Ford would carry on lengthy conversations by radiogram when Ford was away on business trips. Mother would stand with the receiver operator at the Ford Motor Company, and they would chatter away, back and forth, while the operator tapped out the conversation on a teletype machine.

There were two different worlds at Ford—the Rouge plant and the Farms. Ford Farms included the Village, the museum, the engineering lab, the test track, the airport, the farms proper, and related buildings. Harry Bennett was the Rouge, and Mr. D.

and Mother were the Farms. Bennett was Jesus at the Rouge, and Mother and Dad were a combined Jesus at the Farms. And Mr. Ford was God. So say the men who worked for Ford.

You would hardly know that Henry Ford was considered some kind of god, however, from the humble way he played with me—or should I say the diffident way. I remember he taught me how to twiddle my thumbs. And he could make his thumb disappear—another great trick if you're five years old.

In those days I had a large model railroad set on a big table top, about 10′ x 20.′ I was playing with it one day and the signal wouldn't work. My trusty friend Mr. Ford fixed it. He was always coming over and fixing shorts in my railroad or finding out for me why it wouldn't run on a particular spur.

One day, when he had fixed it after I had tried mightily and failed, I looked up at him and said, "Gee, Mr. Ford, you're a genius." I think that was the hardest I ever heard him laugh.

4

"The Little Prince of Dearborn"

Mother once found a thousand-dollar bill Ford had been using as a bookmark. I don't remember whether she tried to give it back to him or what happened to it. If she did try to return it, he probably said, "Finders-keepers," or words to that effect.

Maybe he planted it there as a surprise for her. It would be typical of him, on a par with the way he had surprised me by planting the car key at my plate on my fifth birthday.

I think I must have been about thirteen years old when Ford sent me to cash a $25,000 check for him. Casually, just like that. He needed some cash. I jumped into my car and went to do his errand, going to a bank at Dearborn, as he had suggested.

I grabbed something to carry the money in, something that I recall looked like a little lunch box or a tool chest. I thought nothing of it and returned back safely with the money.

Only later did I learn that he had sent a security man to drive along behind me and I had been covered all the time. I don't know why he sent me on this errand; knowing Ford, I think it might have been to see how I handled myself, how reliable and honest I was. Or it may have been that he just wanted me to get used to handling large amounts of money.

But also, knowing how secretive Ford could be about his cash and cash dealings, I suspect he just may not have wanted any of his aides to see that particular check, and he knew it would have little significance to me. As a matter of fact, I cannot for the life of me remember who the check was from.

I know that many wealthy men ride around without a penny in their pockets, always expecting someone else to pay for the little things. Henry Ford was not one of them. He liked to carry lots of money, and he always paid cash.

Mother tried to instill in me a healthy respect for money, but it was hard to do when a kindly old man was showering me with gifts. Anything I wanted was mine, even things I didn't know I wanted until after I saw them.

I know now that Ford was humoring himself and having fun when I was a child, bringing things to make my eyes light up. If I wanted anything and my mother said no, I had only to wait till I got Mr. Ford alone to confide my secret wish with a long, sad face.

Sure enough, pretty soon Mother would be getting the thing for me. It was like pressing a magic button, and I learned how to push it cleverly.

Sometimes I got my kicks getting something ahead of the Ford grandchildren. Benson and Josephine might say they wanted a certain kind of mechanical toy, and I would slip around and explain my need to Mr. Ford and wind up getting it first.

Ford was a reasonably good driver and had even driven race cars; but in his sixties, when I knew him, he preferred to have someone else drive—maybe for greater security, maybe for companionship, or a little of both. I remember one driver named Wilson.

It really was ironic that Mrs. Ford was scrimping along and darning his socks and her own underwear, while Henry was spending all that money on toys, yachts, planes, horses, and anything else that struck his fancy. His car was specially outfitted.

It had a hidden gun fitting, and it was a moving arsenal at times. It also had a little bar for teetotalers which kept Poland water at a certain temperature. I hated to get thirsty in the car, because Ford disapproved of drinking anything refrigerated and believed his good health depended on drinking water that was slightly warm—body temperature.

I recall that one of Henry Ford's last personal cars was equipped not only with the usual bottle warmer but with the earliest prototype of directional signals. It also had an early two-way radio, collapsible seats, and a footrest for relaxing while sitting up.

Almost anything Mr. Ford had, I had—and it was free. Ford, Dad, and I used the same barber, Al Oliver. He would come to the engineering building especially to cut our hair. He would leave his shop and come to a room that was set aside as a barber shop.

When Dad was at the plant he didn't eat in the dining room with the minor executives, but in one of the special dining rooms set aside for more privileged people. Almost every time that I had lunch with Dad, Mr. Ford would suddenly appear and join us. I don't know how Ford knew I was there.

Many times he would suggest that I come back on Saturdays, too. That was when most of the executives were off and Ford felt the most uninhibited. Those Saturday luncheon sessions were great for my ego. I was always included in the conversation, even if it had to do with business about which I knew next to nothing.

Ford got a tremendous kick out of asking my opinion. Some of my answers amused him greatly. Once I told him something I had heard around school. It was about how God was dead.

"God made the world and all the creatures of the land and sea in five days," I said. "And on the sixth day he made man. But on the seventh day he took a look at man and died laughing."

Ford and Dad looked at each other, not knowing whether to laugh or scold. So they did neither.

Once I was sitting on the bank of the Rouge with a pole and a can of worms—the Rouge was clean in those days.

Ford came by and said, "John, catching anything?"

"No, sir," I said.

"Why not go over to the pond at Fairlane. You might have better luck."

Just then I felt a tug and couldn't handle it. Ford took the rod and landed the fish—a huge catfish. "Whatever you do, John, don't tell Firestone I caught a catfish." Harvey Firestone was a trout and salmon fisherman.

Immediately afterwards he had the river stocked so that his grandchildren and I would have some good fishing. But the fish didn't seem to like the company of the catfish and never stayed around very long.

My parents and I always had access to the Fords; there was never a time that it was impossible to get to Mr. Ford. We had a private telephone line to Fairlane.

He allowed my parents to give me anything I wanted (within reason), and added to it by giving me things as well. At one time, I wanted a car built. It was going to be a 1941 custom-built Lincoln Continental. Mother had approved it and had the chassis ready to be sent to California. Louie Welch had an engine-rebuilding plant out there, and he and my father conspired. They sent back word that Coach Craft would not be able to fill the order; due to wartime shortages, certain metals were not available to complete the body.

Later I found out that the real reason they didn't want me to have it was that it would have been a better car than Edsel Ford, the president of the company, had at that time. After the war,

"Henry the Tooth," as the men around Henry Ford II called him behind his back, had my plans duplicated and made into a car for himself.

They screwed it up. Something was wrong with the balance, and it never handled properly. It was being repaired in the experimental garage every other week. Poor Henry.

With all the special treatment and special attention I was getting, no wonder I was nicknamed "The Little Prince of Dearborn." At least it was better than being called a bastard. However, I did not know about the nickname until years later, when I ran into an old friend from Village days. He said, "How's the Little Prince of Dearborn?" I growled, "Who the hell are you calling a little prince?" and he said, "Didn't you know? Everyone called you that."

For a kid, I guess I did carry quite a bit of loose money in my pockets. It must have been hard for some of my playmates who didn't have my resources.

At the 1933 Chicago World's Fair, Mother gave me ten dollars to have fun; I rode the dodge-'em cars all day. Even at ten, cars were my whole world. At the 1939 World's Fair I spent twice as much, spending the day riding the flying turns, the roller coaster with no rails.

Once I went swimming with a bunch of boys in the Swanee River in Greenfield Village. When I got back to shore the forty dollars I had had in my pocket was missing.

I must have been about twelve or thirteen at the time. We all had a pretty good idea of who had my money, and we searched him, but the money was not in any of his pockets.

Later his father returned the money. It had been in the kid's shoe. His father tried to straighten him out, but he ended up afoul of the law on a more serious charge as an adult.

Henry Ford had two sides. For the most part he was not a kind man. He was hard as nails, tough and ruthless. But to his friends he showed a human side.

At our house he was relaxed, easy, comfortable, and approachable. I was made aware that he was a giant of the times, but *he* was not the one who made me aware. He didn't wear his success as a badge. I was never really ill at ease with him unless I found myself in some trouble.

On one Halloween some friends and I took a BB gun and shot out some streetlights on Garrison Road in Dearborn. I was caught along with my friends, and we were taken before the police chief, Fred Faustman. I thought that after my parents were notified and I was punished, it was the end of the matter. Two days later Mr. Ford sent for me in Dad's office and asked what it was all about—he had heard I'd been picked up for destroying city property.

I said yes sir, I had been, and I was sorry. "I don't want to hear anything like that about you again." His voice was very stern, and then it softened. "Do you hear me, John? Never again."

His grandson was no angel either. Once little Henry II purposely opened the chute which let the oats down for feeding the horses. He left it open, and a barnful of oats came through. Mother caught him and gave him a swat on the seat of his pants. The men had quite a job getting the oats back up.

Mother did not start out by putting me in Henry Ford's school. At first she enrolled me in a Catholic school called Gesu, which was part of the University of Detroit. But I was not even permitted to finish the first grade there. Mr. Ford objected. He did not want me to go to a Catholic school, and he wanted me at Greenfield Village, where he could keep an eye on me. Mother and he argued about it.

If there was anything Henry Ford disliked as much as Judaism, it was Catholicism. I have heard him rant and rave about both Catholics and Jews. Mother was a Catholic, but he pretended he didn't know it.

Mother would get up very early and go to church before

Mother dressed in her flying gear. In 1927 she was the first licensed woman pilot in Michigan. She and Dad were both learning to fly at the same time, but she beat him to the punch and soloed while he was away on his cross-country trip in the Model A.

Dad and I at Dearborn, in 1927, just before he started his cross-country endurance run with the new Model A. He was accompanied by Mr. Ford on the first leg of the trip, then went on to the Pacific Coast, New York, and back to Dearborn. It is remarkable that so little has been written about this trip and its importance to the promotion and subsequent sale of the Model A. The entire trip took eighteen days and covered a distance of 7,580 miles.

Greenfield Village claims to have Henry Ford's baby bed. Not only do *I* have his baby bed, but his cradle as well. A diary written by my nurse attests to the fact that Mr. Ford gave both to me on May 29, 1923.

Mr. Ford gave me this aluminum replica of the Fordson tractor; at the age of six months I had my first personal exposure to mechanized transportation.

That's me on the ore-carrier *Henry Ford*. Even before 1925, Henry Ford's philosophy of self-sufficiency and total control was reflected by the company's providing and transporting the raw materials necessary for the assembly line.

Buddy pulling my scaled-down pony cart. Josephine (Dody) Ford is in the driver's seat, Billy Ford is in the wagon, and I'm standing next to them.

My 1923 Fronty Ford racer, which finished at Indy in 1930, when I was seven years old. It had been specially modified with a built-up seat and extended pedals so I could drive it.

What a surprise! As he left, with only a handshake and a "happy birthday," I thought that Mr. Ford had forgotten to get me a gift. When I returned to my seat at the party table, next to my plate was the key to this motorized, miniature car.

Most boys dream of going to the circus; I had the circus come to me. Another birthday present from Mr. Ford: Snowball, a trick horse from the Ringling Brothers, Barnum and Bailey circus.

Dad (left) and Mr. Ford wait with hats in hands while I take a rest on the Scotch Settlement School steps. Henry Ford attended this school as a boy and later had it moved to Greenfield Village. This picture was taken at its

original site, just before the monumental task of moving the building, foundation and all, was begun. I later attended the same school and sat at the same desk that had been assigned to Mr. Ford so many years before.

Three paintings by Irving Bacon
depicting Mr. Ford's boyhood. I posed
for the young Henry Ford.

Ford arrived on Sunday morning, as was his habit. If she didn't get home before he got there, he paced around or looked at the newspapers; it was made to look as though Mother and I had just gone out for a little air. But of course he would have had to be blind not to notice that we were all dressed up.

Ford would have been even more upset had he known that a relative of ours had some Jewish blood. It was an irony of his life that the man who was sued for his bigoted statements against Jews was always running into people of Jewish ancestry.

Sometimes Henry Ford knew they were Jewish; sometimes he didn't. All I know is that once in a while when I was with him and some of the other men would say about the person under discussion, "Did you know he's Jewish?" Ford would say, "That's all right, he's not full Jewish. He's just part Jewish."

Pressured by Ford, Mother took me out of the Catholic school about halfway through my first year and enrolled me at Greenfield Village. That was, I believe, in 1930, and I went there through ninth grade, in 1939.

Henry and Benson were not great in school, and I was as poor a scholar as they. About the time Henry the Tooth was giving up on Yale, I was making Ds in prep school at Deerfield Academy.

Henry Ford was paying for it, as he paid for everything, indirectly. Now and then came those notes signed Henry Ford, urging me to do my best and keep up the good work. Mother saved them all, and I'm glad she did, because I have new respect for the man's strange genius.

I realize, looking back, that I disappointed Ford when I did not do what he wanted and stay near him; but I escaped him to try to lead my own life by going East to school.

However, much more than life at Deerfield Academy, I remember life at the Village school when I lived in the constant shadow of Henry Ford. I vividly remember the little Scotch Settlement School, how it felt to sit in Henry Ford's own desk and how exciting it was to have the airport right across from the school. In those days so few planes came in that having the school and airport so close together was not considered a hazard.

At one time the Ford trimotor was the most frequently seen airplane. One day one of the planes caught fire in the air over Dearborn. They weren't sure where it would land, and Dad had to rush over and evacuate the school. It missed the school and crashed at the airport; the pilot and copilot were killed. I had rushed over and arrived in time to witness the crash.

Now and then we had another kind of tragedy around school, usually the death of a dog or a horse which was part of the Village atmosphere. But one morning we learned that John Ekles, the WJR radio station announcer who worked on our school program, had committed suicide.

I might have been in the fourth or fifth grade at the time, and I had been the last student announcer the day before he died. I took a lot of ribbing about it, the kids maintaining that I had driven him to it. I even now cringe at the morbid humor kids accept.

Interestingly, Henry Ford felt that we schoolchildren should have experience both in front and in back of the microphone at a very early age as training for a possible future career. Our school program actually went out on the air like any other local show.

It originated from the Martha-Mary Chapel. The school announcer changed every week, to give turns to as many students as possible. I was one of the youngest announcers, and I may have been one of the favorites, because my voice was so deep. That may also have been the reason I was chosen at such an early age. I would say I was used a little more often than most of the kids.

The program tied in with our morning chapel service. I would read a few psalms and then we would have the singing of a few hymns or songs like "Red Sails in the Sunset," "The Isle of Capri," and others that were Ford favorites. Ford might be watching the recording from a distance and beaming a little.

Looking back, I am reminded of an old biblical patriarch, nodding his approval and enjoyment of the local entertainment offered for his pleasure.

Mr. Ford hated the church-on-Sunday routine. His car had been stolen right in front of the church one day while he was inside. But what had turned him against churchgoing, as a final straw, was a minister who had preached a whole sermon one Sunday aimed at getting Ford to part with enough money to build a new Episcopal church.

That was exactly the wrong way to get money out of a stubborn man. As Ford explained at our house, "I told him it was no soap." When my mother asked Mr. Ford whether he hadn't relented just a wee bit and given a small contribution to a building fund, he replied sheepishly, "Oh, I may have given him a little envelope."

The little envelope, my mother found out later, had contained several thousand dollars. But Ford stayed away from his church as much as possible.

Sundays he spent with us, arriving early, staying late, wandering in and out. And all the rest of the week, to my discomfort, he shared the church experience every day with the whole student body of Greenfield Village at the Martha-Mary Chapel, where student attendance was mandatory.

He would sit in the balcony, where he could see who was there. I was most annoyed, because I was not too fond of church myself, and I could have gotten away with missing the service, except that he might have reported to my mother.

Looking back, I realize these assembly moments were very dear to him, as they now are to me.

My bodyguard-chauffeur, Carter, drove me to chapel. Dad would usually bring Mr. Ford or pick him up after the service. When I was thirteen I drove myself to school. The chapel, incidentally, was named for the mothers of both Mr. and Mrs. Ford. His mother was the Mary; he had gallantly put his wife's mother's name first.

If the reader finds it hard to believe that the world's most powerful auto tycoon would bother about who went to chapel and who didn't, read this note from Mother's diary:

Wednesday, March 4, 1936
64th Day, Ember Day, 302 Days to come

Boss called from Georgia about ten, told me to have Ray around office at 3. He'd call again about prices, etc., on a shovel like our big one. Gus and Schroeder asked about a Root Cellar.

Boss called at three and said he'd call at 7:30 again. Did and said he had pictures of kids in chapel and about 20 missing, to find out who they were and let him know. Said the weather was fine—and to send milk order Friday.

It was Mr. Ford's habit to spend some time alone with me every Sunday. Sometimes he would arrive in his electric boat, which he kept at Fairlane. He would come gliding silently up the Rouge River to our farm, which was across Ford Road.

He would take me on a ride up the river and then down the river and back to our place; that would be my Sunday boat ride.

I can remember several times when he got hung up on the branches that had fallen in and of course would come back and report this to Dad. Immediately on Monday a crew was out cleaning the Rouge River.

It was pretty well maintained, but every time there was a storm, the branches would be strewn over the water. That was one of Dad's many responsibilities—seeing that the Rouge was neat so Mr. Ford's boat had smooth sailing.

It was on these boat rides, when Ford had me all to himself, that he did his best preaching to me, a captive audience. He tried to instill his principles and prejudices into me; these included watching out for monied Jews and Catholics, studying hard at school to take my place in the Ford Motor Company, and not getting involved with girls.

Ford had a favorite quotation which he repeated to me many times to fire me with a desire to reach my goals. It was from Longfellow, and it went, "Still achieving, still pursuing. Learn to labor and to wait . . ."

They were words he lived by, and he wanted them to be mine.

Once Ford's quiet electric boat brought him along at the wrong time. It was well known that Mr. Ford didn't approve of drinking or smoking—which certainly was not true of his staff.

In the 1930s it became fashionable to have "roundups," as they were called. Occasionally Dad and Mother would throw one of these shindigs on a Sunday.

It usually would start with harness racing; Dad, of course, had many harness horses. They would invite their various friends, most of whom were company VIPs; a few were outside friends. Those who liked to race the sulkies would hold a real race on the harness track, with an excited audience, betting and all. I don't recall Harry Bennett, one of the top men and Dad's competitor, doing much harness driving, although he could do it. Instead, he and Russ Dawson, a Ford dealer, and Harry Mack, who was in charge of the dealers, would ride horseback on the bridle paths.

Some would race and some would ride the horses, and some would sit around gossiping about Ford plant news. Usually great amounts of beer and booze were consumed. A buzzer was set up so that Dad could be warned if Mr. Ford was coming over.

There was a watchman at our front gate twenty-four hours a day, and if Ford drove over or rode up on his bicycle, the watchman would punch the buzzer, which was connected to a bell on the barn that could be heard at a good distance. By the time Mr. Ford got from the front gate to the roundup, everything would be in order—the cigarettes would be in the fire and the liquor whisked away and replaced by lemonade. But this particular day, instead of coming over by bicycle or car, Mr. Ford came over in the boat and started walking from the river toward the roundup.

Luckily I happened to be riding at the time and saw him walking through the field. When he was still a good distance from the party, I took off like Paul Revere as fast as I could to warn Dad that the British were coming by boat *and* by land—and even now he was swinging through the flats.

57

Fortunately everything that even suggested booze was put away by the time he arrived. But from that day on they would run a constant check with one of the servants at Fairlane to make sure that Ford was still home and wasn't approaching by boat.

Organized religion was not the only thing Ford had qualms about. He was also none too impressed with medical doctors. Ford himself preferred a chiropractor, Dr. Lawson B. Coulter. As a matter of fact, he had Coulter come to the school early every morning to attend to any ills we kids had. Mother was in charge of making sure that Coulter was paid for his services, but—strangely—she was almost cruel in withholding his pay. The amount of money he received was pitiful—something like $35 to $60 a month.

His best month, I see by the records, netted him $63. But for some reason—maybe she didn't approve of him—Mother let the bills run from month to month, and he would send her pleading and threatening notes. At the bottom of one bill which had been running for six months and now stood at $287, the poor man had written, "I have counted on receiving this money at end of each month since December to meet payments. A check would be greatly appreciated. L. B. Coulter."

The bill was dated in February. I see that Mother finally got around to paying it April 14.

On another bill which had been dragging for seven months and had reached a grand total of $329, the doctor resorted to a veiled threat that he would go over her head:

Mrs. Dahlinger:

Am in need of this money, if I do not hear from you by 10th of April I will take it for granted that you wish me to send the bill to the office.

L. B. Coulter
(signed)

Since the bill was addressed to Mr. Henry Ford, the hint is that the matter would be taken up with him or his secretary, and

I'm sure that Mother must have gotten a check off to him right away.

Ford liked Coulter. As a matter of fact, if Ford had a cold or didn't feel well, he would come to the school during the clinic hour, just like us kids.

Though Ford was hero-worshipped by many, he himself was the greatest hero worshipper. He collected heroes, inviting them to his home and bringing them to Greenfield Village School so that I and all the other children could be inspired to greatness.

Thomas Edison was his top hero, and Ford even bought a winter home in Florida next door to his.

As I recall, I met many of the world's great, even before I quite understood why it was an honor to know them. There was Madame Curie; Charles Schwab, one of the wealthiest steel men in America; and the Prince of Wales, whom I understand I waved at when I was just a little tyke.

Henry Ford was very insistent that I get to see the Prince during his Grand Tour when he was causing young ladies to swoon all over America.

This is Mother's diary from the day of that famous visit of the glamorous Prince (Fairlane refers to Ford's private railroad car):

Oct. 14, 1924

Nice warm day like spring. Awake at 5:30. Slept off and on till 8:30. Miss Lynch got up with John. Bathed and went to the plant. Arranged curtains in private car, Fairlane, for trip next week.

Home, changed dress and met Ray at 1:00. Had lunch and chased back and forth awaiting the Prince of Wales. He came about 3:10. We met them on Townline near Michigan. Archie was driving.

The Boss, Edsel, and the Prince sat in back of open touring Lincoln. Had lunch at house and came out where we saw little engine like at fair, then went around and into engineering building where we danced old dances. But Billie, the player, had gone home and couldn't dance.

As the Prince was coming out, Newkirk had gone and gotten Miss Lynch and John. John recognized the Boss when he came out. John waved, so did the Boss and the Prince waved, smiled and tipped his hat. We then came home and read and were in bed at 8:30.

Henry Ford entertained not only a prince but also various presidents. I met President Hoover, Will Rogers, Wiley Post, Joe E. Brown, Mickey Rooney (when he played young Tom Edison), Gene Raymond, and Joe Louis, the "Brown Bomber."

I remember that Thomas Edison was the first person I knew who was hard of hearing, and I was fascinated by his ear horn. I saw him many times.

When I met Charles Lindbergh, shortly after his flight to Paris in 1927, he was the tallest man I had ever seen. Until I saw him, I had thought that Henry Ford was the tallest man imaginable. Actually Ford was just a little taller than Dad, who was 5'9". But Ford was wiry and thin, so he seemed very tall. When Lindbergh stood beside him, however, Henry Ford seemed dwarfed.

Mother was involved in many of Ford's adventures with the famous. Here is an excerpt from her diary at the time the Edison movie was being made, using Greenfield Village and Menlo Park for location:

> Sent Polly and Jerry Wolf to NY to bring back the Boss's first car and motor, which he wants here for a picture they are making of Mr. Edison's life, in which Mickey Rooney will play Mr. Edison as a boy, when he was put off the train at Smith Creek, when a chemical exploded in the train, with which he was experimenting. Met Mickey Rooney and he is a swell kid. Spencer Tracy is here now and he will take the part of Mr. Edison as an adult.
>
> They are making the picture in the Village and are using the old Sam Hill Engine with the cars. Met Tracy and he also is a swell fellow. Weather is rather cold and they are postponing shooting the picture until it is nicer.

I met the great aviation pioneer Igor Sikorsky when he landed his helicopter on the lawn in front of the museum at the Village. I remember being impressed by his hat. It was not the exciting aviator cap with ear flaps that Mother and Lindbergh wore, but a large-brimmed hat that he wore with the brim up all the way around. Sikorsky was donating his first successful helicopter, the V-300, to the Henry Ford Museum.

Among the few things I learned very well at Ford's little school at Greenfield Village were mechanical drawing and how to print. Ford was very pleased. A course in drafting was mandatory for all boys. If any of us had talent for eventually becoming designers of anything—including cars—Ford wanted to make sure we were ready to express our designs on paper. Not having had such a course in his own youth, he had a hard time putting such things down.

One year Mr. Ford decided that the senior class should try its hand at building Model Ts. He set up a small assembly line, and all the senior boys worked on the cars. Even though I was four or five years younger than the rest, he arranged for me to be part of the assembly line.

The seniors resented the little kid who was given special privileges, especially since Mr. Ford would arrive and discuss the assembly problems with me. I would answer with great dignity, and I did not disappoint the Boss. When there were serious technical problems and everyone was stuck, I was usually the one who came up with the solution. I was amazed to learn that not all kids were mechanically inclined.

This car-building project was a one-time thing for the first graduating class at Edison Institute, which was the high school at Greenfield Village. Each boy got to keep one Model T that he and his classmates had built.

Inspired by all the leadership I saw around me—Mother's, Mr. Ford's, and Mr. D.'s—I decided to assert myself too and to make changes around the school. I tried to get a student council started that would make rules without interference from adults. I decided I didn't like the principal of the school and tried to get him fired. I talked to Mr. Ford about it, and he said, no, he thought the school was doing a good job and the principal had better stay where he was.

I wanted to leave school. I didn't like the way things were run.

I was able to be a bit of a Santa Claus to my friends at school, courtesy of my Ford connection. I was not a big ice cream lover, but the plant cafeteria was behind the private dining room, and I had access to all the keys. On Saturdays I would take some friends and raid the ice cream freezer.

Mother and Dad kept our boat, the *Evangeline*, at the Rouge plant. Once Henry Ford went with us in the *Evangeline*, and I was surprised to see that we were followed by another boat. The Ford people were not taking any chances on losing their leader in a boat mishap.

There was a boat that every once in a while, for some mysterious reason, had trouble staying afloat. That was the paddle-wheel boat that plied the Swanee River in the Village, and perhaps with a little assistance from some of the school kids it managed to sink half a dozen times a season—never when people were in it, however.

When Dad was late, it was a family joke to ask, as soon as he appeared, "Did the *Swanee* sink?"

I was always under the protection of FMC, as we called the Ford Motor Company, and in my teens I used that fact to my advantage. There were four or five of us fellows who played a game of baiting the cops in the area. My comrades on these excursions always included Hain, Gale, and Dore, who had red cars. I had a V-8 60.

I was only thirteen and the legal driving age at that time was fourteen, but strings were pulled so that I had my license a year earlier than the law allowed. Anyway, four or five of us would tear around corners, each in his own car, until we would get a cop to follow us. Then we would hightail it home and put our cars in the garage. Usually we made it.

But on one particular night the cops followed me and I scooted in one Ford gate—the guard knew me—and out the other. The policemen could not follow.

For games, we played polo on cowboy horses on the infield of the half-mile track, but it never became a really popular pastime.

Ford was not particularly interested in sports, except for the athletic teams at the Village schools. During one world series, however, the Detroit team played the St. Louis Cards, and Mr. Ford brought the St. Louis team out to meet the kids at the Village. His favorite Detroit players were Ty Cobb and Mickey Cochrane.

Ford used to come to watch me swim when I would practice for meets. He wouldn't say much—many times I wouldn't even know he was in the balcony—but when I climbed out—if I was alone—he would simply say, "Keep up the good work," and be gone in another minute.

He liked to ice skate. At the farmhouse we would bank the tennis courts with snow and flood them. On Sundays when Mr. Ford came over, he would sometimes skate. Once when I was out shoveling the rink, Mr. Ford walked over with his skates on and started to help with the shoveling.

When he had finished, he took his first run across the ice and ended up on his fanny, sliding sideways into a snow bank. He sat still for a while, and I began to wonder if he was hurt, but he looked up at me with just a trace of a smile and said, "People who enjoy skating are often down-to-earth people."

Mr. Ford was never happier than when he was talking cars or tinkering on an engine. I remember once when he was all dressed up for some special occasion he stopped to see me.

I was at the barn near the old farmhouse, working on my car. I had sent to California for some Eddy Meyer intake manifolds and high-compression heads. The intake manifold was for dual carburetors. When Mr. Ford saw I was having trouble, he took off his coat and helped me with the linkage.

It didn't matter to him that he had messed up his clothes.

When he was satisfied that the job was done, he left, and not before then, even though his driver came to remind him that a group of people were waiting.

When I was thirteen or fourteen I asked Mr. Ford if I could work at the test track. He said if it was all right with my Dad I could do it. Since it was a school job, I was paid two bits (25¢) an hour just like the rest of the kids.

I was the only kid allowed to work at the test track at that time. Ford said he knew I could do it because I had been driving since I was five years old. But he added, "I want you to stay away from any work that is considered dangerous."

After about four weeks of doing extremely boring low-speed runs, I switched to high-speed runs, and by the time he found out about it, he realized that I was able to handle it. So I was permitted to continue.

He would ask my opinion on what was wrong with the cars I had driven, and I would tell him it was the radiator or the brakes or whatever.

One time, after I'd been test-driving awhile, a radiator blew up right in front of me. Steam covered the windshield.

Ford came over shortly after it happened. It was the first time I realized how much he cared and was concerned about me.

He was extremely upset, and after a few minutes he asked me what had happened. I said, "I don't know. I was just driving the car as hard as I could. It was a high-speed run and the radiator exploded. I don't think it should have, even at that high speed."

"Why did it explode?" he asked, still somewhat agitated.

"I don't know—probably because it wasn't built properly."

He smiled, patted my back, and said, "That's probably right, John."

All the boys who went to the Village school started mechanical training in earnest in the seventh grade. From that time on they worked at least half a day a week either in manual training or in the machine shop, earning 25¢ an hour. Ford provided excellent shops. I remember starting with woodworking, then graduating to the metal lathe. We next advanced to the engineering laboratory.

Henry Ford was delighted that, as he had been in his youth, I was drawn to racing cars. Dad built the test track on which I drove, testing Ford's new model cars.

The test track was built around the Ford Airport, but we also used a portion of both runways for car testing. That was in pre–World War II days. When a plane was coming in, whistles blew and all cars scurried off the runways.

There were many places that I could work during summer vacations. During the summer I was sixteen, between test drives, I liked to drive trucks. I would drive to the Upper Peninsula of Michigan before they started the glider project at the Iron Mountain plant.

Iron Mountain was where they built the old wooden-body Ford station wagons. In the early part of World War II the plant was converted to build gliders for the army. I spent many an hour making deliveries between Dearborn and Iron Mountain.

For a young man, I was doing all right in my summer jobs. I had the excitement of riding around and speeding up to ninety and ninety-five miles an hour, and a weekly paycheck on which grown men in the late '30s could more than raise a family—$200.

Sometimes I would go with Mr. Ford out to Tecumseh or Macon to visit the Ford farms and Ford schools. Most of the time we went with Dad, but a few times we went alone together. Mr. Ford never talked much as we drove. He seemed contented on these drives, as if he liked being away from the plant and with me. He once said to me that his work had become drudgery and all the fun had gone out of it. I said that maybe he should quit and work at the Village and the museum and let Edsel take over. He sharply spat out, "No!"

I was only repeating what I had been absorbing at home. Mother and Dad were always talking about Edsel, Ford's only son, and how much control he should be permitted to have over the Ford empire.

I knew even as a child that something was very wrong and that Mr. Ford wasn't treating Edsel right. That's what Mother said, and I could tell it was true from the things Ford would say about Edsel at our house.

Though I enjoyed being important to an important man, I knew at an early age that I did not want to follow in Ford's footsteps. And what made it especially hard was knowing that both he and Mother were counting on me.

Ford would ask me about school and my future plans as we sat around after Saturday luncheon. I always tried to let him down easy. I'd say, "Well, it's fine, except that I can't go to the University of Michigan, because I'm not learning a foreign language."

He'd say, "John, you don't need a language to become an executive at Ford Motor Company."

I did not dare tell him that I had no intention of ending up at Ford Motor Company, so I'd say, "Yes, sir, but you need a language to get into the University of Michigan and become an engineering student."

He'd invariably reply, "John, by the time you become ready for college, I will have a college for the students of Greenfield Village and Edison Institute."

My heart would sink because I wanted to get away and see the world. But Ford kept his promise—he developed a college, the Edison Institute of Technology, where you didn't need a language. As it turned out, I didn't go there.

Ford's schools trained boys to be of use to the company. That was all well and good, but for me it wasn't good enough. In 1938 I decided that I had to get away. Ford asked me why, and I had to lie a little. I told him I wanted to be a doctor, and to become a doctor I needed a foreign language—Latin. He detested Latin. He didn't like a language that wasn't spoken.

But he said, "If you think you want to become a doctor, and to become a doctor you need Latin, then I guess you'll have to go away to school, because I'll never teach Latin."

Of course I didn't want to learn Latin either, but since it

was my excuse for leaving home, I stuck it out for one semester and then switched to French. But, all in all, it satisfied Mr. Ford that I had a sound reason for leaving Edison Institute. He was not thrilled, however, and when I came home he would ask me how it was going.

I would answer, "Not too well." He'd ask why, and I'd tell him straight out that his schools were a year behind the Eastern schools and so was I. "I don't give a darn about the Eastern schools," he would tell me.

I would infuriate him, at times, by running down his schools, but it never dulled our relationship. As a matter of fact, I got the impression that he always liked me to tell him stuff straight.

5
It Wasn't Easy Being Mrs. Ford

When I was a child of about four and playing with the Ford grandchildren, I used to think that Henry Ford had been pretty dumb when he was building his first car. And I used to look at him and wonder how he'd managed to get so much smarter.

The reason I thought he was dumb, and said so freely—to the delight of the little Fords—was because of the story that the children's Grandma Clara used to delight in telling. Even she laughed at how silly their Grandpa Henry had been.

The story, as she told it, was that Ford was working on his horseless carriage in the barn behind their house on Bagley Street in Detroit, and he hadn't even had the sense to check the width of the car against the width of the barn door. Came the night that he was finishing up and getting ready to test-drive his creation—a mechanical marvel with four bicycle wheels and saddle, gas tank, wires and gears, and hand lever for steering.

He came running into the house to get her and to wake up his little son Edsel so that he too could witness the glorious event.

Mrs. Ford worried a little about the noise that would be made in the middle of the night, but then she had a worse worry. As she watched in horror from the back door of the house, she saw her husband crash through the walls of the barn with a pickax as he enlarged the doorway enough to get his little masterpiece through.

Then he went blithely riding around the block, with the engine putt-putting and spitting through the night air.

History repeated itself years later in the '30s, when Dad built his first Indy car in the basement of our uncompleted house. Not only did the door have to be knocked down; the whole wall had to be removed.

I gradually came to understand why Henry Ford preferred the company of my mother. Mrs. Ford, unbelievable as it may sound, sat around pretending she was still the small-town farmer's wife she had been when they married. She mended her clothes and his, and I remember Mother's commenting once that Mrs. Ford was mending her "petticoats and underdrawers."

One day Mr. Ford was sitting at the table in the kitchen of our old home—the one we lived in before he built a home for us—complaining that his feet hurt. As he wiggled his toes he said mournfully, "I wish she would quit darning my socks. I think I've got enough money to afford new ones." Mother smiled and Dad chuckled.

The schoolchildren in the Village were supposed to be very grateful to Mrs. Ford for the Christmas party she gave every year. There was a party, all right, complete with a midget dressed as Santa Claus, which everyone liked. But Mr. Ford didn't like his wife's miserliness when it came to buying presents for the children.

Naturally, he felt that she could afford to open up and give really meaningful gifts or toys to the children who were, for the most part, sons and daughters of Ford plant workers. But she never did. Instead, Mr. Ford sent Mother to New York to buy additional presents which were a little more in keeping with his idea of what the gifts should have been.

Mrs. Ford's only luxury was her use of customized cars and higher-priced models. She always had a Mercury or a Lincoln, and she used a chauffeur-driven Lincoln with a glass partition. In summer the front part would be opened, and the chauffeur would sit stiffly erect as he rode in the open air. It was the ultimate.

The only car Clara Ford ever tried to drive was an electric car, not a Ford. It was still in the garage before the war, and now and then she would take it out and drive around Fairlane.

Ford had a private train parlor car and sometimes Mother joined him there. He also had a yacht, and Mother was sometimes there too.

From time to time Mrs. Ford would send a message that so-and-so was ill and would Mrs. Dahlinger please arrange a basket of food to be delivered to the home.

Mrs. Ford always called Mother "Mrs. Dahlinger," never Evangeline or Billy. She may not even have known that Billy was her husband's name for Evangeline.

Sometimes Mr. Ford would call and invite Dad and me to lunch. Usually if he took Billy he didn't take Ray. And sometimes I would have him all to myself.

When it was just Dad and me who were invited, we would drive over and pick up Ford, then we would go to the plant and sit at the special table that was always reserved for Dad at the engineering lab complex.

Ford and Mother spent a lot of time walking together, I recall. They loved to walk the railroad tracks; they would start from Dearborn and walk all the way to Detroit on the tracks— a distance of seven or eight miles. No one would ever recognize them, because who would expect to see the great man walking the tracks?

However, at the end of the line, Ford's car and driver would be waiting to take them back.

In contrast, I've been told, as her kind of adventure, Mrs.

Ford sometimes went through old cemeteries looking for old-style flowers. I think pinks were her favorite. She liked old-fashioned flowers like sweet peas and blue larkspur. In spring it was wonderful to smell the lilacs that she had around the house.

Mrs. Ford's whole life in the summer revolved around her prize flower gardens and especially her roses. As long as I can remember, she was the president of her garden club. Any time ladies came to visit her, or even when tycoons and bigwigs came to see Ford, she invited them into her garden to see the roses, rumored to be worth a million dollars.

No effort was too great to locate a particular kind of plant she was after, or to start a new tree or bush from a cutting.

The big deal around the Ford mansion was the arrival of the ladies of the Garden Club. Mrs. Ford had organized it some years earlier, and the ladies never failed to reelect her president. It was her point of pride.

Even as a child I wondered about Clara Ford, what she did in that big house all by herself. I wondered because I knew that while she was all alone at Fairlane, except for servants, her husband was at the Ford plant doing exciting things or at our house with Mother and Dad.

Now and then I would get into one of my little cars and buzz over to see her. She was always good for some milk and cookies. When I crossed Ford Road the cops would look the other way, since I was far too young to have a driver's license.

With her grandchildren I explored the house, banged the piano and spent time in the too-elegant tree house, with its miniature furniture. We children also liked to play the wind-up Victrola.

My favorite spot in the Ford mansion was the private bowling alley. We would bowl and fight over who had to be pin setter. Since this was in the days before automatic pin setters, I was too lazy to bowl in between the grandchildren's visits, because I would have to bowl and then go back and set the pins up myself. I thought of getting one of the Ford servants to do it for me, but I was afraid it would get back to my mother, who would disapprove.

Mrs. Ford was very interested in the morals of young women, and she was connected with a home called Priscilla Inn, where nice young girls could live in dormitory style, well chaperoned. There was another outfit called the Girls Protective League that she also took interest in, and occasionally she would visit wayward girls at the house of correction. She was known locally as "the erring girls' friend."

Mother had to get involved in these matters, because Mrs. Ford kept up a large correspondence with all kinds of benevolent organizations. On and off Mother was considered Mrs. Ford's personal secretary. Sometimes this involved arranging for teas and other social events. Sometimes the ladies would be really clever and meet in colonial costumes. I have a picture of Mother in some such get-up. Mrs. Ford also liked to give old-fashioned costumed cotillions.

Mrs. Ford liked to tell her grandchildren and me about the days when she was a young girl living on a farm and Henry was the best skater in town. We wanted to know if he had courted her in an automobile, and she said heavens no, he had a flashy red sleigh, with sleigh bells that made beautiful music as the horse sped them along to the local pond where all their friends were skating.

But she did point out that even while they were courting, Henry was working on something that would be the forebear of the tractor, using parts of an old wagon and a harrow for the body.

But what had really impressed her and her crowd the most, said Mrs. Ford, laughing, was the time he arrived at a dance with a watch that he had put together so that it had two sets of hands: one for train time and one for what he called sun time. The watch made him the life of the party, and Clara Bryant sat out the dances with him, sensing even then that if she married him, this is what her life would be like—there would always be people clustering around to see what he was up to. He was already talking about a "horseless carriage" that he hoped to build.

Mrs. Ford was a bit annoyed that the public thought her husband had been penniless when he married her and that he had been a pauper when he built his first cars. The truth, she said, was that her husband had earned a nice income from a saw-mill he operated and that his father had given him eighty acres as a wedding present with enough lumber to build a house.

Being a real go-getter, Henry Ford had gone to work with a will and built the house before their marriage, which took place in the spring of 1888.

It was a square house, and Clara Ford loved it and would have been content there forever, but her husband was very restless. While she was playing the piano one day, he took a sheet of her music and sketched a prototype of a gasoline automobile, showing her how it would work and pleading with her to move to Detroit. She knew it was hopeless to refuse, because he would go anyway, so she packed her favorite wedding present, an old English clock given to them by Henry Ford's father, William Ford. And off they went.

Finding a house had not been so easy, said Mrs. Ford. But they scoured Detroit and finally found exactly what they needed on Bagley Street. It wasn't the house or the address that thrilled Henry, but an old red brick barn behind the house that Henry could use in his spare time for his inventions. For his full-time job, he went to work for the Edison Company.

He was in his late twenties or early thirties then, and little did Clara dream that one day the owner of that company, Thomas Alva Edison, would be their dearest friend and they would buy a home in Florida at the Edisons' insistence and spend every winter with them.

Henry Ford had become wealthy enough to give her back her square house and have it restored to the way it had been when they were honeymooners. It was not too far from Fair-lane or our house, and I kept my ponies and horses in its barn.

Josephine, the only Ford granddaughter, said she bet her grandmother cried when she went to see the square house, because she had been heard to say she wished she had never left there.

Henry, Benson, Josephine, Billy, and I thought the square house was pretty neat, too, but we enjoyed the run of the big house because it had some features dear to a child's heart. It had several bays (or towers, as I thought of them) that were fun to explore. Henry Ford seemed to think so too, because he had a hideaway in one of them. We were not allowed to touch anything in there.

Whenever he was home, we knew that we could find their Grandpa Henry there. But Ford was not one to just sit and think. He was always tinkering with something or sketching some possible auto engine. He would take time to answer our questions or talk cars, but I seemed to be more interested in mechanical things than the other boys.

I remember that Mrs. Ford was always ordering the cook to serve lamb chops for dinner. That had been what Edison liked to eat, and anything that Edison liked was all right with the Fords.

The Edisons were the Fords' closest friends for many years. After Edison died, Ford relied more on Dad and spent more time with him. For a long period Harry Bennett, security chief at the plant, was also Ford's close friend. But he left before Ford died. Actually, in Ford's last years, he had very few close male friends except for Dad.

There were Ford relatives, of course, but outside of the family no one but the Dahlingers and Bennett were privy to his relaxed thoughts and conversation. I am sure, though, that we Dahlingers knew more about what was going on in the Ford family than some of the closest relatives. And we also knew more about Henry Ford's thinking and his plans than they did, because he used Mother or Dad as his sounding board.

He would sit at our house complaining about how his family did not understand what he was trying to do for their own good. And though he himself caused a lot of their jealousies and dissensions, he would deplore them and complain bitterly about them.

I remember a perfect example. Ford had bought a tremendous

yacht and spent something like a million dollars fitting it out into a lovely pleasure craft for his family.

But then came World War I, and he patriotically donated the craft for military purposes. When Ford got it back, he started to fix it up again but got annoyed because all the family was squabbling over who would get to use the boat. As Henry put it, "I had to teach them a lesson." He ordered it cut up for scrap, and he never got another yacht like it.

But what he did have was an electric boat and all kinds of smaller boats. I was glad that Mr. Ford never did the spiteful things to us that he did to his family. He certainly seemed to be almost a different person with us.

Ford didn't have a hell of a lot of tenderness, but I got the feeling that he liked having me around, and that was sometimes enough to give me a nice feeling of security.

I never saw him display affection with his wife or kiss her; his calling her Callie probably seemed evidence enough of his affection.

Only with Mother did he seem to unbend a little more. But so formal a man was he that everyone called him Mr. Ford. He was not the kind of person to call Hank. People close to Edsel did not call him Mr. Ford, but rather Mr. Edsel, and that's what I called him too.

The closest thing to tenderness that I would see in Mr. Ford would be the look on his face when he talked about his own mother, who had died in his youth.

There was one particular memory that haunted him, and every time he saw a bird's nest with a bird sitting on eggs or could lift me up to peep in at the bird's eggs, he would react in the same way. The memory that he held dear was of a time his father had cut down a tree in the barnyard, and lo and behold, there was a nest with eggs in it and two very upset sparrows.

His mother had held him while he leaned over the tree trunk and peered into the nest. His father had held young Henry's little brother, John, so that he too could look into the nest.

I remember another incident with birds, one that I witnessed.

It happened when I was about eight, but I remember it as if it were today. Mr. Ford was sitting on a stump, his back to me, looking out over the Rouge River and playing a jew's-harp as if he had an audience of thousands.

He didn't know I was behind him, and I guess he thought that he was alone. When he had finished, all you could hear were the sounds of birds, and he took a little bow. Not exactly a bow; he nodded his head to the birds. It was sort of a special moment that I'll always remember.

Ford had a thing about jew's-harps. He thought they were wonderful. He always had a couple in his pocket and more in the car. If I didn't have mine with me, he would give me another. And he was always handing them out to little kids around the Village.

He could play the jew's-harp pretty well—at least a lot better than I could. Sometimes he would sit and twang one while he waited for Dad. Sometimes he would keep me company when I was little by working away on the jew's-harp while I worked away digging dirt with my shovel. We must have been quite a sight.

Mrs. Ford was not a great dancer. Mr. Ford preferred to dance with Mother, who was naturally athletic and was great on the folk dances that Mr. Ford loved. Dad would dance with Mrs. Ford while Henry Ford danced with Evangeline. Of course Mr. Ford would do the proper thing and start off the dance festivities by dancing with his wife, and Dad would dance with Mother.

I danced with Mrs. Ford too on occasion and, in little-boy fashion, would carefully pick a dance where I would be safe from having a toe stepped on.

Ford thoroughly enjoyed bouncing about in the folk and square dances and even the colonial dances. He was very agile and limber for his age—or anyone's age.

Ford was not very sophisticated in his taste in music. He had a fine piano. For himself, he enjoyed the fiddle and played it fairly well. At Fairlane there was a dance floor that the Fords used for their old-fashioned dancing.

Sometimes, Mother, Dad and I would be clowning around with Mr. Ford. He would grab his fiddle, Mother would accompany him on the piano—not too well—and Dad and I would strum away on jew's-harps . . . what cacophony! You could hardly recognize the song.

It didn't matter. It was almost always the same song—his favorite—"I'll Take You Home Again, Kathleen." It was a bitch to play on the jew's-harp. Whenever I was walking with Ford for any length of time, he would start humming it. I remember once Dad was driving him to Edsel's house at Grosse Pointe and I was with them.

He almost drove me crazy humming that song over and over. He wanted me to learn the words so I could sing it with him. I remember his saying that "I'll Take You Home Again, Kathleen" was also Edison's favorite song, which seemed to explain everything.

I made a mental note to try to forget the words that I already knew of the song, because singing a duet with the hummer was at the bottom of the list of things I wanted to do.

Maybe the reason Mrs. Ford concentrated so on her garden was that she hated her famous house, Fairlane. It now is a museum. It had a museum quality even back then. It was surely not a house meant for comfortable living.

It didn't matter to Mr. Ford. He was at his plant or out on inspection or at our house most of the time anyway. But it mattered to Clara Ford, who was marooned in a castle. All she needed was a moat, and it would have been complete isolation—had it not been for her hordes of lady friends from the garden club. There were gatekeepers, and one had to state one's business to come through. It did discourage anyone from dropping in, and I think Mrs. Ford was a lonely woman, eager for company.

Maybe that's why she sewed and mended and walked among her rose beds. She also spent a lot of time writing instructions for Mother. Mother did most of the shopping for Mrs. Ford, and Mrs. Ford would tell her things she wanted to find or complain about something that Mother had gotten.

There were a lot of notes about bread. When the Fords went

to their summer place, Mother had to send many loaves of Mrs. Ford's favorite bread at one time, and there would be complaints or praise about how the bread had kept.

Fortunately, Ford was a great believer in day-old bread. He would not eat fresh bread, maintaining that it was bad for one's health. I remember he would preach to me about the dangers of soft hot bread—it was worse than poison. He kept a supply of his bread at our house, as well as other things he liked.

He hated chickens and said they were unfit for human consumption because they ate worms and bugs. Pigs, too, were beneath contempt for their eating habits. At least cows and sheep ate nice clean grass.

For a time, he preached that sugar was dangerous, that it chewed up the stomach because of the sharp edges. He had sounded the alarm after looking through a microscope and seeing that sugar resembled ground glass.

Then someone in the lab had tried to dissolve his fears by squirting a little water from a dropper on the sugar under the microscope to show that all the sharp edges disappeared. Ford did not permit his myths to be destroyed that easily. He still distrusted sugar.

I am forever amazed at how frequently Ford came to right decisions for the wrong reasons.

In his own way, Henry Ford was a health nut. He did not drink. Strangely enough, Mrs. Ford did drink, moderately. She liked her snifter of Cherry Heering, and Mother had to order it for her—by the case. She also liked an occasional bottle of Rolling Rock beer, which came in pony bottles of seven or eight ounces. Dad would order a truckload from Pennsylvania.

Her husband paid no attention to her liquor consumption, but he wasn't quite so tolerant when it came to Edsel. He attempted to have spies keep an eye on Edsel to see exactly how much he was drinking. It wasn't easy to do, because Edsel's wife, Eleanor, had managed to spirit him away to that haven of auto tycoons and the social set, Grosse Pointe, more than an hour's drive away, in an attempt to break the stranglehold Ford had on her husband. Mrs. Ford approved. She knew that if Edsel lived closer, Henry would be on his neck twenty-four hours a day.

Mother was a lot like Ford, maybe because of his influence. She didn't drink or smoke. She stayed very slim and youthful. Mrs. Ford, possibly because of the beer she enjoyed, became what was called pleasingly plump.

Mr. Ford did have a weakness—watermelon. Mother knew she could bring a sparkle to his eye and a smile to his lips by serving watermelon, no matter what the season. She would have it trucked in from the South in winter to surprise him.

Frequently there would be a phone call announcing that Mr. Ford was coming over for tea in the late afternoon. There would also, just as frequently, be watermelon.

Henry Ford had personally chosen most of the colors and decor of Fairlane, and the interior was frightfully dark. The huge sitting room, where Mrs. Ford spent most of her time, was Henry's pride and joy; very dark stained wood, very expensive. Mrs. Ford was always apologizing for how dark it was. Mr. Ford would say it looked all right to him.

That was supposed to close the subject, and it did. But one day, when Ford was gone on one of his frequent trips to check on his many plants or dealerships, she ordered some workmen to paint it white. When Ford got home he was furious, but he didn't say anything. Instead, he came to our house and discussed the matter with Mother, threatening to have the paint scraped off and the original finish restored. Mother took Mrs. Ford's side, trying to explain women's rights.

Only Mother could get away with snapping at Henry Ford and telling him off. Had she been a man, he would have fired her. But as it was, he seemed to enjoy being able to squabble around a bit with someone in a give-and-take way. That is not to say that Mother was always tough with him or hard to get along with.

Not at all. It seemed to me, as a child, that much of the time she treated him with a great deal of respect, seeming to hero-worship him and asking his opinion on all kinds of things that

I knew she had already made up her mind about. She also knew how to be coquettish, looking at him soulfully with her large hazel eyes. Ford warmed to her. He would sit in his favorite chair talking on and on about what he believed or what she should do about this and that.

It was amusing to me that Ford would say that he couldn't stand a person because he talked too much. But as far as I could see, he did an awful lot of talking at our house, and everyone else was supposed to listen.

To show you the kind of woman Mother was, she once planted an apple orchard on Ford Road just west of Greenfield; parts of it are still there. She also planted on Michigan and Gulley Streets. When I asked her why—I was seven at the time—she said, "Because it will look nice."

It wasn't even our property, but she wanted it to look nice. She was a law unto herself. It was so typical of her to simply take charge and do something or order it done without getting permission and making a big deal of it.

Getting back to Henry Ford and his health regime, he would drink nothing but Poland water, and I still have a few bottles of it around from the supply he kept at our house.

Ford believed that the way to stay healthy was to move fast. He was wiry anyway, and to see him stepping along and bounding up steps even at the age of seventy was like watching a wire spring on a screen door jerk shut.

Thomas Edison disapproved of cigarettes and said they were bad for you, and so Henry Ford, who took everything Edison said as gospel, declared that cigarettes were bad for you. He was 'way ahead of medical science on this point, even though he had nothing but Edison's word to back him up. Ford would walk around his plant trying to catch someone smoking. And if he caught them, they were fired.

Mother would carry large sums of money, $100 or $200, so that if she saw something Mrs. Ford would like, she could just buy it. Because of the money she carried for Mrs. Ford—and also to buy things for Henry Ford now and then, such as leather goods, memo pads, and pocket secretaries—Mother applied for and received permission to carry a gun. It was a neat little thing that fit into her purse, and I'm sure that if anyone had tried to hold her up, she'd have blasted him between the eyes.

Every so often Mr. Ford and she would be busy at target practice. One of our employees would run and change the bull's eye and hover around nervously while all the shooting was going on.

I loved guns. They didn't frighten me a bit, and as soon as I was able to hold one steady, Ford brought me my own pistol, and we three practiced.

To my knowledge he himself never shot any animal. He disapproved of my deer hunting because he had a herd of more than a hundred head roaming free on Fairlane.

My mind springs back to an early morning when Ford and Mother were walking around Fairlane and a buck took a sudden dislike to Mr. Ford and knocked him on his rear. Even though he was wearing a gun, he did not shoot the buck. He came hobbling to the house, leaning on Mother. Dad and I thought it was pretty hilarious that the buck didn't realize or care that Ford was the boss and owned him and all the lands the buck roamed.

Dad wiped the smile off his face and offered to go find and kill the disrespectful buck that didn't know which side his bread was buttered on. Mr. Ford ordered the animal shot, and Dad rounded up a hunting party and went after it.

Mr. Ford was not against fishing. In fact, he liked to indulge in this sport. But he was very impatient, and if the fish didn't bite in five minutes, the hell with the fish! Ford was gone.

I have many slips of paper showing what Mother bought for Mrs. Ford and how much cash she plunked down. Here is one, I see, where Mother gave the store $100 in cash and still owed $153.20.

Mother would give Mrs. Ford the list of items and be reimbursed, except for the down payment, which I believe came from Henry Ford. It's interesting to see what prices were in those days as compared to today:

Prices for Mrs. Ford's Suits

Eggshell-brown long coat	$56.95
Brown wool coat	44.50
Brown 2-piece suit	31.95
Eggshell 2-piece suit	31.95
Black/white 2-piece suit	22.95
Navy-bleu suit	33.95
Pink 2-piece suit	30.95
	$253.20
	100.00 paid
	$153.20

Signed: Mrs. Ray Dahlinger

(Notice that Mother, who was French Canadian, still used the French spelling for *blue*.)

Perhaps some readers would like to taste something that was used at the Ford home. This is the recipe for the sausage that Mrs. Ford regularly had made up by her staff, and I believe Mother had our cook make it up in batches as well:

Sausage (Strathy Hall)

        6 lbs. lean pork
        3 lbs. fat pork
     12 tsps. powdered sage
        6 tsps. black pepper
        6 tsps. salt
        6 tsps. powdered mace
        2 tsps. powdered cloves
        1 grated nutmeg

Grind fat and lean pork in a sausage mill, stir in seasoning, fry a small piece and try. Make any changes you like.

6
Ray Dahlinger–
The Man
I Called Dad

The year 1977 was the fiftieth anniversary of the Model A. I was surprised that not a word was mentioned by the Ford Motor Company about Ray Dahlinger's role in proving the worthiness of that successor to the Model T. In 1927, with great national fanfare, Dad drove a Model A car cross-country and back. It was not in the same league as Charles Lindbergh's crossing the ocean in solo flight, but Ray Dahlinger's performance crossing the country in the dead of winter, racing against the clock, had its own kind of merit.

Crowds greeted him in the cities and towns along the way. Headline streamers proclaimed his endurance. I have the log of that journey. It shows:

Cross-Country Trip:
Dearborn to Los Angeles

Friday, December 2, 1927
10:05 A.M. Left Dearborn. Accompanied by Mr. Henry Ford as
    far as Saline, Mich. During the first hour we made only 31 miles

owing to slippery condition of the roads; second hour, 80 miles; third hour, 120 miles.

Mottville. Ten minutes.

[Dad would write the number of minutes he stopped after the name of the town where the rest stop took place.]

Saturday, December 3

12:40 A.M. Carbondale. Roads very winding and very rough. Ten minutes. 571 miles.

Sunday, December 4

3:02 P.M. Midland. Washed face in cold water; eyes burning. Fifty-one minutes. 1,674 miles.

Monday, December 5

12:01 A.M. Arrived El Paso. One hour and fifty-five minutes. 1,978 miles.

Changed at El Paso from Central Time to Mountain Time. Lordsburg, N.M. Many cattle and horses on road, which slowed us up a lot. Twenty-five minutes. 2,143 miles.

At 2,145 miles it was snowing badly. Could scarcely see, but passed all vehicles safely.

Tuesday, December 6

1:02 A.M. Arrived in Los Angeles in good shape. 2,987 miles.

Dad was gone twenty-one days, starting December 2 and arriving back in Dearborn on December 23. He started in Dearborn, drove to Los Angeles, then San Francisco, New York, and finally back to Dearborn, a total of 8,328 miles. Dad held the wheel the entire time, except for 532 miles when his relief driver drove while he rested.

I was only four years old when he made this trip, but later he told me that the hardest thing the Model A had to contend with on the trip happened near Tuscola, Illinois, where they struck a hundred-foot strip of flooded highway.

Fortunately the motor did not give out, though they hit the water at fifty-five miles an hour in darkness. In some places the car had to ford foot-deep water. The windshield froze over almost immediately, and they could not see where they were going. They had to spend a miserable half-hour digging at the ice with their fingernails.

Dad's trip was not a test run but a demonstration of the stamina of the Model A in facing every driving hazard. Though Dad went through ice, snow, mud, and sand, he only touched the hood of the car occasionally to put in oil.

The car averaged 40.9 miles an hour, and its gas consumption was a terrifically low 20.1 miles to the gallon.

As a sample of the excitement Dad's cross-country run created, I have a picture of Dad and his car when they seem to have taken the New York financial district by storm. The caption reads:

LIZZIE'S SUCCESSOR VISITS WALL STREET

The new Ford blocked traffic in the financial district yesterday when Ray Dahlinger, manager of the Ford plant at Dearborn, drove it to the National City Bank to call upon Gordon S. Rentschler, assistant to the bank's president. Dahlinger in eighteen days covered 7,580 miles from Detroit to Los Angeles to New York. Left to right, Mr. Rentschler, Mr. Dahlinger and Charles E. Mitchell, National City president.

Here is another example of the enthusiasm generated by Dad's trip:

> The Scott Auto Company
> Authorized Ford and Fordson
> Sales and Service
> December 12, 1927

Henry Ford, Esq.,
Dearborn, Michigan

Dear Sir:

In appreciation of the fact that I am the only woman in New Mexico fortunate enough to see the new Ford Car as it passed through our town on its trial run, am sending you some little poems I have composed on the old and new cars.

I am the wife of the Ford Dealer in Lordsburg and had the extreme pleasure of serving hot coffee and soup to Mr. Dahlinger at the Garage at 4:00 A.M., December 5th.

Thanking you for thus infringing on your valuable time, I am,

Yours sincerely,
(signed)

The Test of the "Model A"

Bidding goodby to the homeland,
Leaving the factory nest,
Gleaming bright
In the morning light
The new Ford started west.

Quiet and mild as the moonlight,
Fleet as the rays of the sun,
She left the line
At the hour of nine
All ready to make the run.

Built for endurance and safety,
A blessing to all mankind,
For comfort, speed
And every need
The work of a master mind.

Braving the darkness and dangers
Nor stopping night nor day
She made the run
To the setting sun
Three cheers for the "Model A."

A driver who knew and loved her,
Himself to the great task lent.
To guide her on
From dark till dawn
Across a continent.

Battling colds and blizzards,
Fighting the imps of sleep,

> Night and day
> On the stormy way
> Determined his charge to keep.
>
> With a nerve and will of iron,
> A modern Paul Revere,
> He made the trip
> With never a slip.
> Hats off to Dahlinger.

It was most unusual for Dad and Mother to go anyplace together. Each had a private life that didn't include the other, for about as long as I can remember. First one would be away on a trip, then the other. Usually Henry Ford was involved in some way—he would send Dad off to check on dealerships, for example. He would say that his own face was too well known, but if Dad showed up at a Ford distributorship and garage in, say, Cleveland, he could snoop around and find out how they were treating the public, and no one would know Ford had sent him.

Once while we were all on vacation down in Biscayne Bay, Dad was racing Gar Wood in the 999, a special V-bottom racing boat that belonged to Ford. Dad beat Gar Wood, but in one of the later heats the engine blew and Mother had to fish Dad out of the drink. She sped to the rescue in her boat, the *Evangeline*. Although I was in her boat, I learned about all this later because I was only a year old at the time of the race.

Jimmy Smith was the riding mechanic with Dad, and they were both hurt, but fortunately not seriously.

Mother's boat was a 36-foot speedboat, built by Hacker with a Liberty engine. Mother was very proud of it. It was one of Ford's many gifts to her. She was a sportswoman at heart and loved speed—fast horses, speedboats, and airplanes. With Ford, she got them all.

The Biscayne Bay vacation was the only time I recall that we were all on vacation together. There were times when Dad would join us for a long weekend. Usually it was Mother and

Meme and Pepe—Mother's parents—and I who would go. And, of course, Miss Lynch.

Here are a few samples from Mother's diary, after Mother was married and before I was born. They show the flow of her life and how Ford was involved in it. This is the time when Mother was still eagerly yearning for a child and sharing her husband's bed. After I was born, things were different; they did not share the same room.

The diary begins as the Fords were leaving for their Florida vacation to escape the Michigan winter:

Sunday, Jan. 12, 1919
    Got up early, straightened everything and did all outside chores. Ray only watered the horses and then he and Ott went over to Mr. Ford's house. I followed and arrived just as they were leaving. Ray went to depot and chauffeur took home Trum and the cook. Trum told me about Sato being very bad man, etc. . . . got recipe for white cookies that Mrs. Ford likes. Made some too. Told John about separating chickens.

In the spring, Ford was back.

Wednesday, Apr. 16, 1919
    Rain again. Did more office work and took care of chicks—fed them today. Ray and I went to Gardulskis and Fustnaws and Harts to see about buggy. Ott got his new Easter suit and every-thing. We had pork shoulder steaks, creamed potatoes, and peas.

    Boss called up and came over for an hour or so. After he left we were so tired. I went to sleep on the davenport and Ray in the chair. Finally went to bed at 11:30.

Friday, Apr. 18, 1919
    Sun shining for a change. Boss got me out of bed to say he would be over after a while. Worked around outside and then at three-thirty took Ray's horse, Prince, over to the farm's garage and we went down Reckner Road, around and then home. Took

buggy and drove over to Mrs. Reckner's and gave her $300.00 for her car.

Home to dinner of steak and creamed potatoes. Read awhile. Bed early.

Sunday, Apr. 27, 1919—Je suis malade—
  Nice sunshine today. Boss came over at 9 with sedan and we went to Redford, returned about 12:30. Newkirk, Carl, Eliz and a fellow by the name of Plitch (Newkirk's friend) were here in a big car.

How did Dad take all of this—the fact that Ford was so close to Mother? The romance, if it continued into Ford's final years, was so discreet that I didn't see the forest for the trees.

I think that most of the time Dad was busy with his many projects, and only occasionally did he wonder about it. Most of the time he and Mother had a very close working relationship. They talked about work, sports and me. These were their major interests.

There was a time when I was quite young when he did seem to be pleading with Mother to have one bed and not two. She had taken me to Miami Beach for a vacation. I have a six-page handwritten letter from him dated March 9, 1929, when I was going on six, in which Dad tells Mother how lonely he is without her and expresses his views on the subject:

"You said about twin beds. I think they're made for only sick people, not people that love each other. . . . I wish . . . our room would have *one* bed just for *you* and *me*. Is that alright for me to say that? There goes the kid again. . . ."

Dad seemed to be very deeply in love with Mother. I do not understand all the undercurrents in the letter, and even now I do not want to pry too deeply into his private life. I know that he did love me, too; his P.S. says, "Kiss John for me."

By the time I was old enough to think about it, I don't remember ever seeing any affection between them; it was just a friendly business partnership. They were emotionally isolated from each other.

When my wife, Bette, was talking to one of the men who grew up on the farms, he mentioned that it had been a marriage of convenience—that Henry Ford had arranged it.

It was Ford, really, who kept them together. Dad had great respect for Ford, who had elevated him from a mechanic test driver to a position of importance and trust. Dad was one of the few men around Ford to have an actual title—Manager of the Ford Farms.

But that didn't mean that Dad was only a farmer. He was anything Ford needed. And he was always there when Ford didn't know whom else to trust. When Ford went on his pilgrimage to Europe in 1915 to try to stop World War I, Dad was the man Ford relied on most. Someone once called him "a man for all reasons."

On the Peace Ship, Dad was in charge of one million dollars in cash and gold. He had to carry around vast amounts of cash to pay for all the expenses incurred by the Ford entourage. In addition to that, he was entrusted with the keys to the safe that held the bullion.

The only sign that Dad might have cared more than he let on was that he drank fairly heavily. I don't know whether Ford was unaware of this or if he simply pretended he didn't know. At the various Ford plants, if Ford smelled liquor on any worker's breath, he would pass the word to the foreman to have him fired. Dad was never fired. And his service for the Fords outlasted Henry Ford's life.

Ford had reason to look the other way. He was a lonely man, in a way, and needed the warmth of Mother and Dad and their companionship. He never unbent enough to unbutton his shirt, but at our house he did unbend a little. And he liked the fuss made over him by our guests. Though he was a multimillionaire and eventually a billionaire, he still needed encouragement.

Dad was very patient with Ford, always trying to figure out what he wanted and doing it for him. In a note to Mother sometime before World War II, Dad wrote:

I have been with the boss a lot going over the Edison plant about five to six hours a day. You know how I like it, trying to rush the job and he doesn't let you know what to do. It's hell. But I suppose I have to stand it. Poor boss, if he would tell a fellow what he wants we sure could do it, but you know he doesn't know himself.

Dad was not unattractive, and several of the women who attended the roundups would make a play for him. In fact, the word was that one of the employees' wives "had a thing for Mr. D." With the encouragement of a few drinks, she would start grabbing him and getting quite physical.

Once, to the amazement of my young eyes, I caught them kissing behind a tree.

Ray Dahlinger was not a lonely bachelor when fate and Henry Ford decided he would be the perfect solution to finding a husband for Evangeline. He was practically engaged to one of his sister's girl friends. He was supposed to marry this woman, and he was the most surprised person when he didn't. But when Mother turned on the charm, hardly a male could withstand her appeal.

Dad was in charge of Ford's twenty-two hydroelectric plants. When one of them was being built, Dad had the idea to enclose the pipes in tunnels to provide easy maintenance.

Ultimately it was done, and someone else took the credit for it. Dad mentioned this to Ford, who said as long as *he* knew where the idea came from, it didn't matter.

And as far as Dad was concerned, that settled it. He didn't make a fuss or brag to the other men. It was Ford's good will that meant the most to Dad. To the day Ford died, this was paramount in Dad's mind—that he please Ford. He genuinely liked Ford and Ford liked him.

What sort of people did Ford like? Straightforward people who didn't mince words. He liked people who worked hard—it didn't matter if they were janitors, inventors, or statesmen. Dad had been a floorwalker in a fashionable department store before working for Ford. Ford didn't like cheap people, people who skimped when they didn't have to. He liked kids because he could trust them. He didn't trust too many people.

Dad had a lot of clout because of his relationship with Ford. One sign of his importance was his own private table in the executive dining room, though it was not in the same inner sanctum where Mr. Ford had his table. Nor was it where Ford's other close friend, Dad's sometimes friendly, sometimes fierce competitor Harry Bennett, ate.

I'd better explain further. Bennett, Mr. Edsel, and Charles Sorensen had their offices at the Rouge plant administration building. Henry Ford's office and Dad's office were at Dearborn, several miles away.

Across the way from Dad's office was the experimental garage, in one section of which was the executive dining room. There Dad's private, round dining table was located.

Bennett's office was in the basement of the Rouge administration building. Ford liked to hold some of his own meetings and appointments there because he could more easily escape. If he didn't like the person who was arriving or didn't want to see him or her for any reason, he could sneak out the back door which led to the garage and make a fast getaway.

How different language sounded in those days! Mother had her own pet phrases; her favorite exclamation was "Hot puppies!"

The favorite expression around town and I suppose the country in those days was "Oh boy!" or "Boy oh boy!" Both Mother and Dad gave it a different twist by saying, "Boys oh boys!"

Mother had one phrase that told what she thought of someone: "That mutt." Almost everyone was a mutt at some time, and the word was even used affectionately, as in, "Oh, you mutt," or "Oh, you little mutt, you." I'm sure Henry Ford must have found himself in her mutt category now and then, too.

Around men, Ford was known for his salty language. It was

said that he was like the preacher who could keep a sermon going a full hour and never repeat himself. Except that when Ford was "preaching" at someone, it was to cuss him out for something.

I didn't have the chance to hear much of that, but once in a while when I was just a child I would come upon him unexpectedly and delight in hearing this "man talk."

In his latter days, he toned down and became much less profane.

Dad was a great horse lover, and his stable of harness and riding horses was well known. When a colt was born the day I was commissioned, he named it Ensign John, after me and my rank, and the horse came up a winner. I still have the *Detroit News* dated June 13, 1950, which shows that the horse merited a headline in the sports section. No wonder! The horse was the "longest longshot," and only $90 was bet on my namesake's nose.

As the story lead said, next to a picture of the horse, "Ensign John paid $201.80 straight in winning the ninth race at Northville Downs Monday night. It was the longest price ever recorded here."

As Dad grew older, he turned to racing horses instead of boats, but back in 1924, I see by old telegrams, he was very much in Edsel Ford's good graces for his boating exploits.

One of Dad's jobs was to supervise the landscaping gardeners—passing on Mrs. Ford's orders—so Mrs. Ford's garden would be the envy of all her garden club friends. One year she wanted to set an example for the farmers of America of how they could have an attractive roadside stand to show their wares, instead of the ugly sheds that distressed her so. You might say that in her desire for beautification of the highways she was the forerunner of Lady Bird Johnson.

I have the picture of Mrs. Ford's dream roadside market on a little brochure that was handed out at the National Flower Show on March 17, 1928. Under the picture it says, "Designed and built by Mrs. Henry Ford." The message inside the brochure is short and sweet:

> This model is made out of old boards and whitewashed, and so cheap no farmer can say he cannot afford it. With thousands of miles of good roads the farmer can make more money from a neat attractive building than he can from the ugly-looking shacks we see along our beautiful highways.

7
With Henry Ford in War, Peace, and Politics

People who know that I was close to Henry Ford, if they are old enough, ask about Ford's Peace Ship. They want to know the truth about this strange phenomenon that preceded America's entry into World War I. Could a man exist who had the vanity to think that he could single-handedly stop a war or keep America out of one—a man who was not president of the United States or even secretary of state?

The answer is yes, he could, if he was a man who had Ford's tremendous ego and had an army of men whom he could order around via the "generals," the executives of the Ford Motor Company.

As a matter of fact, there was a rumor going around the Ford plant in my youth (one war later) that Ford had jokingly said he could send over some of "the boys" to "take care of Adolf Hitler." "The boys" could have meant Harry Bennett's security force, or it could have meant other strong-arm men available. Even perhaps the Mafia—Bennett had some Mafia connection.

There were those who thought that Henry Ford should run for president. And there was an effort to draft him for office back before my time—in the 1920s and earlier.

He did make a serious run for the Senate and lost by only a few thousand votes. That's an interesting story, and I'll get to that soon.

As for the Peace Ship, which was also before my time, Ford had permitted himself the luxury of thinking he had grown so high in the affections of the nation, the president, and the world, that he could go riding off on a ship—the *Oscar II* replacing the traditional white charger—and save the world.

At this point, 1915, Ford almost had the right to think he had superhuman powers to influence the world, because he was treated like a god. He had become a hero the year before by announcing that he would pay five dollars a day as a minimum wage, an unheard-of thing when most men were earning from half to two-thirds the amount. He had cut the workday from ten hours to eight. And he had lowered the price of the automobile to under $500, was supplying almost half the total output of automobiles for the whole industry, and was even giving $40 rebates to happy customers who had been assured a rebate if total Ford car sales reached a certain goal.

I heard about the famous Peace Ship, the *Oscar II*, not only from Mr. Ford, when he became nostalgic at our house, but from my Dad, who was along as the trusted bagman to dispense the money as needed. With one million in gold, Ford was ready to pay any man or group of men who could stop the war—if he could find the right men in the warring countries.

World War I had started in Europe in the summer of 1914. The Peace Ship was organized late in 1915. Ford had said, "I will bring the boys home from the trenches by Christmas." He was referring to the American volunteers who were already fighting in Europe. But he also wanted the sons of the European nations to eat their Christmas dinners at home. It was a rosy picture he painted.

Ford was at the center of a whirlwind of preparations for the great peace mission, and it was all systems go!

Another great statement he made was, "The people of Europe are all sick of the war, and all Christianity must join in endeavoring to stop the useless, senseless slaughter of their best."

Ford later gave Mother the large certificate authorizing him to make this trip. It seems to be a special passport, about 14″ by 20″. Either Mother had it framed or Ford gave it to her framed. It is most impressive.

In the upper right-hand corner is a small photo of Henry Ford and the legend, "Good only for six months from date, unless renewed by a diplomatic or consular officer."

The rest of the document states:

The person to whom this passport is issued has declared under oath that he desires it for use in visiting the countries hereinafter named, for the following objects: Norway, Sweden, Denmark, Netherlands.

Object of visit—attending conference. This passport is not valid for use in other countries except for necessary transit to or from the countries named unless amended by an American diplomatic or principal consular officer.

The United States of America,
Department of State,

To all whom these present shall come, Greetings;

I the undersigned, Secretary of State of the United States of America, hereby request all whom it may concern to permit Henry Ford, a citizen of the United States, safely and freely to pass and in case of need to give him all lawful aid and protection.

Given under my hand and the Seal of the Department of State at the City of Washington the third day of December in the year 1915 and of the Independence of the United States the one hundred and fortieth.

Robert Lansing

Description: Age: 52 years
      Stature: 5 feet 10 inches
      Forehead: Medium high
      Eyes: Gray

Nose: Prominent
Mouth: Medium
Chin: Round
Hair: Gray
Complexion: Fair
Face: Medium Round

Mother had a similar document for Dad, and it is interesting to see his description and how it compares to Ford's.

Description: Age: 29 years
Stature: 5 feet 9 inches
Forehead: High
Eyes: Blue
Nose: Prominent
Mouth: Medium
Chin: Round
Hair: Blond
Complexion: Fair
Face: Round

In his youth Mr. Ford's hair had been dark. So was Edsel's, and so was mine. Henry Ford also had a wave in the same spot as I have, and he once commented about this to Mother.

When he was first organizing the Peace Ship, the auto magnate gave Woodrow Wilson a chance to get in on the glory. Ford went to see President Wilson with his wonderful idea of how a nonaligned group of concerned persons could stop the war in Europe by providing a forum for arguing instead of fighting.

Pompously, Wilson said he would be willing to help bring about peace if both sides sent representatives, but he was not willing, he said, to consult with just one warring faction. He was not willing to sit down with just one nation.

Ford was a man of action. If the president was not willing to negotiate for peace, he, Henry Ford, would do it himself. He would bring the peace forum to Europe and he would take with him the most respected men and women on the American scene.

Many big names promised to go and then backed out—Jane Addams, for one, who is remembered for founding Hull House.

The guiding light of the project was an Austrian woman, Rosika Schwimmer, who claimed to have important papers that proved Europe was ready to end the war. She had failed to get to President Wilson with her papers, but evidently they impressed Henry Ford enough for him to become involved in her project.

The *Oscar II* sailed on December 5, 1915; it was, in its stated purpose, a fiasco. There were 160 persons on board, and dissension was rife. Henry Ford was drenched by a wave while taking his daily constitutional the second day out. He developed a cold and hid away in his stateroom most of the time.

A London reporter who was along dared to say in stories sent home to England that Ford was not suffering from la grippe at all, but that he was tied and locked in his cabin.

Madame Schwimmer quickly became unpopular on shipboard because of her air of mystery and the fact that she kept those tantalizing secret documents with her at all times and would not let anyone look at them.

The fortune in gold that was carted along in the hopes of buying off the Germans was never used. The war continued and the United States was drawn in. But the Ford Motor Company gained a million dollars in free advertising.

Dad kept his own running account of the Peace Ship goings-on. Here are some of his loose notes on life on the Good Ship Peace. The reference to President Wilson and "Galting" referred to the fact that while in the White House Wilson had become a widower, and was then courting a handsome young widow named Edith Galt. Their engagement had been announced two months before, on October 7.

• Boss a good sailor. Up early ate good breakfast. 300 miles from Nantucket—heavy seas. Mayor Blankenburg of Philadelphia presented the peace flag to Boss. It's white with large five-pointed star in the middle. Boss quiet and thoughtful throughout the ceremony.

• 600 miles—see by ship's paper that President Wilson is going to marry Mrs. Galt. One joker said that he supposed the President would be "golfing and Galting." Took the Boss's message to Congress up to the wireless room, also took message for Jane Addams who could not join us because of sickness. Wind from the N.E.— ship nose into the sea—tons of water pouring on deck. Much seasickness aboard.

• News conference cancelled. Boss is sleeping. Took daily message to Mrs. Ford, Wm. J. Bryant, Thomas Edison and J. Wanamaker up to wireless room. President Wilson's message to Congress was read to the group. Boss suggested they have a few days to think about it and discuss it—at the deadline all groups could sign a statement condemning the attitude of the President. Everybody talking at once. The meeting ended with the singing of "How Dry I Am" and the waiters got busy.

• Much arguing on board. Everyone for peace—it's just how to get there. Ordered more security for Boss—concerned about cranks harming him. There is a big rumor about Boss asking for financial accounting from Lochner and Mme. Schwimmer. Not true. They have followed Boss's orders and have been turning in vouchers and explanations right along.

• At Orkney Islands, Kirckwall. Boss and I stayed in cabin all day—no visitors. Passed through mine field with tugs to show the way. Boss in cabin with sore throat and cold.

• Boss better and went on deck. Can see Norway and snow on mountains. Captain Hempel gave farewell party. Gov. Hanna of N. Dakota said Boss had done what he could do to stop the war and they asked for three cheers.

• Reached Christiana and it is 12 below. Went to Grand Hotel— Mr. Ford not feeling well.

• Boss has the flu.

• Homeward bound. On steamer—left from Bergen. Sent message to group still in Europe from Boss. He said he would return if he was elected delegate to a neutral conference. Glad it's all over; some nice people but some nuts too. Boss quiet and disappointed but not too bad.

Ford saw no sign that Germany had any intention of settling for a negotiated peace. He arrived back in New York on New Year's Day, 1916.

He was a disillusioned man, certain of two things: that America would go to war and that the way he could help most was to develop a submarine chaser.

He quickly went into the production of tanks, submarine chasers, airplane motors, and other weapons of war. He was quoted as saying, "I hate war so much that I am willing to enter this one to make it the last." Still sorry that his peace mission had failed, he assured the world, "I want peace and I will fight like the devil to get it."

I think Dad thought at the outset of the Peace Trip that Henry Ford could really do what he set out to do, and that Dad would be some small part of a great moment in history. Well, Ray Dahlinger didn't help save the world; he didn't even save himself from marriage.

By the time Dad sailed off into the horizon with that million dollars in gold safely stashed in the hold, plus an additional amount of cash carried in a small inconspicuous suitcase, he was already committed to Evangeline.

How much Henry Ford had to do with getting Mother and Dad together and for what purpose, I'll never know. The romance between Evangeline Côté and Ray Dahlinger was in full bloom about the time of the Peace Ship adventure, and about a year later, in February of 1917, they were married.

Mother always cherished the gift that Ford brought her when he returned from the Peace Ship journey—a large silver brooch set with six large moonstones. It is very beautiful. I still have it.

The United States has never had a great industrialist as a president, but it might have had. There was very serious talk several times, before I was born, of nominating Ford for the presidency.

The story that was given out as the official reason Ford refused to run was that his wife didn't want him to. Clara Ford rather liked her supposed role as political king-breaker. She said that she had warned him not to run because he could not make speeches—he had not had a proper education.

True, he had only a grade-school education, but that hadn't

stopped him from becoming the world's first billionaire. I vaguely recall Ford's talking about his possible presidency in one of his kitchen talks at our house, and my impression was that had he thought he could have made it, he would have taken a crack at running the country.

One hopes he would not have run it in the high-handed manner he ran his company, and would not have tried to do the work of all the cabinet officers as well.

I recall Ford talking to me once as we sat on some steps outside the kitchen. From his comments I could see he felt he might have done a pretty good job as president. The only thing I can remember for sure is that he said if he were president he would get rid of prisons and put all those prisoners to work. He felt the only solution to crime was proper employment.

I think Ford really did have second thoughts about not having tried for the presidency. Surely he must have known that a president does not have to write his own speeches. As a man who had a secretary write out any formal statement to the press, he must have known that he was already operating in the manner of a United States president.

No, it must have been some reason other than having to give speeches or his wife's disapproval that kept Ford from a grand try. Maybe he did not want to invite too close an inspection of his private life. Maybe he didn't want to curtail his private life and live only a public life, in the constant glare of publicity.

Ford loved toying with the press and planting stories, but he also liked being able to retreat into privacy again. Once I read that Ford had left a couple of reporters sitting and waiting for him in the middle of an interview and returned after two hours, saying he had gone skating. He might very well have gone skating—he often did go with Mother and me.

Ford would leave people waiting and would come to our house across the way from Fairlane for a little while, then show up wherever he had started from—someone's office at the plant, or his own home.

Though Ford did not run for president, he did run for the

Senate, and it was a small disaster. As some enemies laughingly put it, "He snatched defeat from the jaws of victory."

It had started on such a high note, with President Wilson calling Ford to Washington to thank him for his war efforts and to say that he was the only one who could save the Democratic Party in Michigan and keep the Republicans from having a majority in the Senate.

The amusing thing is that Ford was a Republican. But Ford's ego was big, and he loved the excitement of the 1918 race.

Ford's opponent was Truman H. Newberry, who came from the place Ford so hated—Grosse Pointe. The Republican candidate had a fine background of public service, having been secretary of the navy for a time; like Ford, he was a multimillionaire.

So they were fairly evenly matched. Polls were taken that showed Ford ahead, which possibly made him a little complacent. That is the only way I can explain what happened next.

On the Sunday before the election, the opposition put out a scurrilous story and newspaper ad accusing Ford of harboring a German sympathizer in his plant, which was then making Liberty motors for the war. Even more damaging, the Republicans claimed to have a statement from the highly respected Charles Evans Hughes confirming this.

The whole thing made it look as though Ford were sabotaging the war effort. It's interesting in the light of Watergate and the dirty politics of the '70s to read a bit from the full-page ad which ran November 3, 1918, in the *Detroit Free Press:*

Henry Ford and His Huns

Carl Emde, a German alien and a German sympathizer, is boss of the drafting work on the Liberty motor at the Ford plant. Henry Ford knows he is a German alien and a German sympathizer, but he refuses to take him off this work.

This is not hearsay. It is absolute fact, vouched for by Charles Evans Hughes, whom President Wilson appointed to find out why the production of American aeroplanes has been so much delayed, when the American soldiers in France need them so much. . . . Mr. Hughes is a former justice of the Supreme Court of the United States. His reputation and respect for the truth and for fairness in judgment have never been questioned, even by his bitterest adversaries.

Concerning Emde's job, Mr. Hughes says in his report to the President:

"It is possible for one in that department to bring about delays the causes for which, in view of the multiplicity of drawings, it would be hard to trace. . . ."

How many American lives have already been sacrificed in aeroplanes tampered with by German agents? If Henry Ford puts so much faith in the German Emde after all he knows about him, is there any reason why he should not put the same faith in the German Hohenzollern? Since Henry Ford is so fond of this German pet of his, is there no place in his large establishment where he can give Emde work and keep him out of the way of temptation to serve his fatherland, as many other Germans have already served in this country? As Mr. Hughes says:

"There has been a laxity at the Ford plant with respect to those of German sympathies which is not at all compatible with the interests of the government. . . ."

It is now plain to every voter in Michigan that Henry Ford is no more wary of Hun agents than he was when he followed Rosika Schwimmer to Europe on the peace ship three years ago. He is as innocent as ever.

If Carl Emde wishes to make plans and photographs of the Ford plant or the Liberty motor for use by the enemies of the United States, Henry Ford is willing to give him a chance to do it, just as he fell for Madame Schwimmer's pro-German peace plans.

Henry Ford loves Huns too much to be trusted with a seat in the Senate of the United States and help make peace with them. Commander Newberry knows them for what they are and is helping to fight them at every stage of the game.

There can be but one choice for wide-awake Americans in this election.

Everyone around Ford urged him to come out immediately with a fighting statement blasting the Republicans and defending

Emde as a patriotic American (he was a naturalized citizen) who worked night and day to turn out Liberty motors as fast as possible and who had, in fact, improved the motor.

But Ford seemed more interested in talking with Emde and assuring him of his faith in him than he was in getting the counterstatement to the newspapers.

Helping Ford with his campaign was Edwin Pipp, who had been editor-in-chief of the *Detroit News*. Pipp warned that every minute's delay was critical, but all Ford could think of was, "I want to tell Emde not to worry." By the time Ford's long statement was sent out, it was too late for it to get as big a play in the country and small town newspapers as the Republican accusation had.

Ford lost by 7,567 votes. A recount was called and the margin was reduced by over 3,000 votes.

This incident, too, may have been a reason that Ford said, "History is bunk." He knew the truth about Emde, and he saw no proof that former justice Hughes had ever made the damaging statement attributed to him.

Ford was still smarting from his unfair treatment and loss of the senatorial seat when the *Chicago Tribune* wrote an editorial, which was widely circulated in other newspapers as well, casting aspersions on Ford's patriotism and claiming that he consorted with anarchists.

Now finally Ford was roaring mad, and he filed a million-dollar suit against the *Chicago Tribune*. The case came to trial—not in Detroit—but in Mt. Clemens, where it was felt the jury would not be influenced by the noted newspaper.

It was the heat of summer, 1919, and Ford squirmed nervously and whittled with his knife as he was wont to do. In an effort to show Ford up as a country bumpkin, one of the lawyers for the defense suddenly asked Ford to tell the jury who Benedict Arnold was.

Ford's answer went down in company history. He looked at the lawyer and said, "Arnold? Why, Arnold was a writer."

Later, after the newspapers and the public had had a good

laugh at Ford's not recognizing the name of America's most notorious traitor, Ford insisted he had thought they were referring to a man who had done some writing for the company and was now dead.

But that was just theatrics. The bottom line was that Ford won the case, and the *Trib* was ordered to pay damages—six cents! When I was growing up, there still were arguments about whether this had been a major victory for Ford or whether it meant that the worst thing one could say against Henry Ford could only injure him six cents' worth.

Ford was starting to see at last that he couldn't fight the power of the press. The press had had its fun with him long enough; he was going to get in on a little of that power himself.

As a result, Henry Ford dabbled in the newspaper business. About four years before I was born, he took over the *Dearborn Independent* and ran it right from his plant in Dearborn. From what I heard the folks say about it, it was mostly a house organ and an ego trip for the Boss, to disseminate his pet views.

He overreached when he started, almost immediately, to publish excerpts of a notorious anti-Semitic work, *Protocols of the Elders of Zion*, written by a white Russian named Serge Nilus. The work had originally been published in London, I believe, and had been thoroughly discredited there.

The articles ran for about a year and a half in the newspaper, but Ford, not satisfied with the number of people he was reaching, went a step further and published the series in book form under the title *The International Jew*.

When I was four years old, in 1927, the whole thing exploded in a million-dollar libel suit against Ford, based on an article which claimed that a Jewish organizer of farm co-ops was the leader of a Jewish plot to capture control of all American farming and farm produce.

The man Ford had tangled with was a Chicago lawyer or grain broker or both, Aaron Sapiro. The suit was filed in United States District Court in Detroit. Ford's defense was that the series had not injured anyone. He also claimed that he had not been the only one to fear "the international Jew" and that the editor of a Jewish newspaper who had gone along on the Peace Ship had also expressed such sentiments.

That man was Herman Bernstein of the *Jewish Tribune*. Ford said that Bernstein had told him on shipboard that World War I had been caused by "the international Jews."

Bernstein and Ford had a confrontation out of court in which Bernstein not only denied that he had said such a thing on the Peace Ship, but stated that Ford's articles and books had incited pogroms against the Jews in European countries. Ford challenged Bernstein to prove it, saying that if Bernstein could find evidence that any Jews had been hurt because of Ford's printed matter, he, Ford, would apologize.

While Bernstein was in Europe gathering evidence, a mistrial was granted because of jury tampering, though it was proven that Sapiro was not involved. The case was set for retrial. Bernstein returned from Europe with evidence that so impressed Ford with the damage he had done that he made a public apology, promised to retrieve all the copies he could of the anti-Semitic book, and settled with Sapiro out of court.

He also repaid Bernstein for the cost of his European trip. Sapiro refused any money except legal costs.

Ford quit publishing the *Dearborn Independent*, and the world was spared any more tirades against Wall Street capitalists and Jews by Henry Ford.

Ford had had it. He was through with newspapers. He was through with Democrats. He came out strongly for Herbert Hoover both the first time he ran and in his disastrous bid for a second term. In fact, Ford went on the radio to try to help him get reelected, which may have accounted for Hoover's poor showing.

Ford hated everything about Franklin Delano Roosevelt except his secretary of the treasury, Henry Morgenthau. Ford said he was glad the nation's financial affairs were in the hands of a Jew.

By the time Hitler began making inroads in Europe and taking over the weaker countries, I was old enough to take a more personal interest in what was going on. I was fifteen when

Henry Ford made the mistake of accepting the Grand Cross of the German Eagle in 1938.

From the way it sounded around our house, Ford hadn't given the little chunk of metal that much importance. He was accepting it more to annoy FDR than anything else. And for a second reason, if he needed one, he was trying to keep good business relations with Germany, since Ford had a plant there.

I remember the folks laughing at Ford's saying he could get rid of Hitler by sending over some of "Henry Bennett's goon squad."

When Ford became disenchanted with Hitler, for his continued land grabs beyond the Polish corridor, he also became disenchanted with Fritz Kuhn, who was on the Ford payroll as a lab technician. Kuhn was called the "American Fuehrer" for his connection with the German Bund. After he left Ford, Kuhn was indicted on a charge of embezzlement of Bund money; he was convicted in 1939.

When World War II came, security measures were taken so that not just anyone could enter Ford Motor Company plants or property. Henry Ford personally signed a card making sure that I would, as usual, be free to come and go. I am looking at one of these cards now, number 807, dated October 23, 1942:

> You are authorized to pass the bearer of this card, Mr. John Dahlinger, thru any of the institutions named below, for a period of one year following above date (Sundays and holidays excepted):
>
> > Greenfield Village
> > Ford Motor Company's plants
> > Fordson Coal Co., Stone, Ky.
> > Henry Ford Hospital, Detroit
> > Lincoln Motor Company, Detroit
>
> > > Henry Ford
> > > (signed)

One man whom Ford considered an enemy was Pierre Du Pont. He said the Du Ponts were running the country and influencing FDR in the days before World War II. The fact that a Roosevelt son had married a Du Pont seemed proof positive to him of an unholy alliance between the two families.

To show how strongly Ford felt about Du Pont, he told us frankly that he refused to be a part of the NRA (National Recovery Act) because Pierre Du Pont was part of it and claimed to have been its architect, at least in part. Du Pont had made a special personal appeal to Ford to display the NRA Blue Eagle as a sign that he was conforming with the code of fair practice as set up by the New Deal.

The special appeal had been like a red flag to an enraged bull. Ford refused to go along with the prewar code that was supposed to bring the nation out of the Depression by the industries' voluntary conformity on prices, wages, and length of work day.

Charles Edison, Thomas Edison's son, was at this time acting as an intermediary between Mr. Ford and FDR, explaining each other's views through carefully couched diplomatic letters which are in my possession. He was especially trying to arrange a meeting between the two, feeling, overoptimistically, that on a one-to-one basis they would find themselves in accord on the more important issues.

Ford was the only auto manufacturer who failed to go along with NRA. On the other hand, it is said that Ford was the only manufacturer who gave back to the government all the profits he had made during World War I. However, I later heard from Mother and Dad that no record was ever found by the government that he had returned the $29 million.

That was typically Ford—the only man I knew who, as the Bible says, surpasseth all understanding.

As for the Peace Ship, I remember Ford's justifying it years later, saying, "At least I tried to bring about peace. Most men don't even try. I make no apologies. Most people are too lazy to do what they should do and follow their own beliefs."

Though his Peace Ship did not sail back with a peace pact, in Ford's defense he did point the way for the League of Nations and the United Nations which were to follow.

8
Up from
Tin Lizzies

The way Henry Ford told the story, the race for a practical horseless carriage had been between the electric car and the gasoline-driven one. Ford said he had always put his faith in gasoline and steam, ever since he had sat for hours as a little boy watching his mother's teakettle on the stove.

He had once tried his own experiment with it, plugging the hole and letting it heat until it blew the lid. It had been a good demonstration of the power of steam, and his mother had been very understanding. She was also understanding about his next experiment, in which he tied down the lid of an earthenware teapot. Hot water and pieces of pottery flew all over the room, one of them cutting a gash in his face.

Actually, it was only by the grace of God and the fates that be that Ford became an automotive enthusiast and not a jeweler or watch repairman.

His first love had been watches. He used to love sitting in the kitchen of our house with his coat off and his glass of Poland water at hand, talking about those early days. He would study his watch sometimes as he talked.

As Mother and I sat listening, I was absorbing a few things that I planned to do based on his experience—especially, become independent.

As Mr. Ford told the story, looking back from the vantage point of his late sixties, it all started with his hatred of "hard farm labor." His early life was spent trying to get away from the farm. And when he couldn't do that, he decided instead to mechanize farm labor, using the steam engine, so that farmers would be liberated. And, more particularly, *he* would be liberated.

The story starts, really, with Ford's mother, who died when he was not quite thirteen. He was always wistful when he talked about her. She had meant everything to him and had been the only one who understood his love of machines. Everyone else around the farm had laughed at him and considered him a "queer duck" because of it.

But while others saw humor, Ford's mother listened solemnly as little Henry explained how he had figured out something mechanical. She even told him that he was a "born mechanic" and encouraged him to keep going and not pay attention to the other boys.

As far as I could see, he followed her advice to the end of his life, never bowing to the opinion of others or changing his plans because of it. In fact, when he would tell Dad to snoop around and see what the men in the plant or some of his executives were saying about something, he would always add, "I don't give a damn *what* they are saying; I just need to *know* what they are saying." What he meant was that knowing how they felt would help guide him in bringing them around to his way of thinking. He seldom changed to theirs.

Ford was fascinated with watches, had many of them, and was always giving me another watch. He would say, "Oh, you don't have your watch," and he'd hand me another one.

One of the first things he had tried to fix as a child was a neighbor's watch. He chuckled as he commented that he'd ended up with more parts than he had started out with. His tool, he said, had been the first thing he had made for himself— a tiny screwdriver made from his mother's darning needle without her permission. She had been very understanding and not angry and I am sure that this incident, too, influenced him in his worshipful attitude toward her memory.

After his mother died, Ford stuck it out for two years, spending all his spare time tinkering, while his father, so unlike his mother, grumbled that he hoped his son would outgrow his foolishness.

His brothers had no such wild dreams as his and grew up eventually to take their place in the community, making good farmers and local officials.

But two years without his mother's encouragement was all Henry Ford could stand, and at the age of fifteen, without a good-by to his father or brothers, he set off down the mud roads toward Detroit, hitching a ride on a wagon whenever a kind-hearted farmer would stop.

With him he had his most cherished possession, and the one he was counting on to help him earn a living—his mother's darning needle turned watchmaker's tool.

He got a job, young as he was, repairing watches in a jewelry shop on Baker Street in Detroit. His pay was fifty cents a day. Because Detroit was an expensive place to live, he came up half a dollar short every week. Room and board came to three dollars and fifty cents weekly, and that didn't include such niceties as shaving cream.

He arranged to work nights, to bridge the gap, becoming an apprentice in a machine shop that repaired steam engines. By working night and day and sleeping when he could, he managed to remain solvent and put a few dollars away out of a combined total of five dollars a week.

His great dream, he would say, directing this part of his story at me, as if urging me on to dream my own impossible dream, had been to be able to manufacture a thirty-cent watch that would be within the means of all the average people. This would indeed have been a bargain, since at that time a pocket watch was at least a dollar.

He didn't succeed in building that utopian watch, and in a few years, when he was exhausted from overwork, he went home, was welcomed back, seemed to settle in, fell in love, and thought of marriage. To set him up and induce him to stay on the land, his father gave him some timberland that he could farm if he would first clear off the timber.

His father was sure that he had outgrown all that foolishness of monkeying around with watches and engines. But to the surprise of William Ford his father and the whole town of Springwells, Michigan, Ford still did not farm but instead set up a sawmill, sold lumber, and—horrors!—built a machine shop for his tomfool experiments.

Surprisingly, Henry Ford started to make money. He operated a portable steam engine for hire. He was called here and there around Wayne County to repair other people's steam engines.

And the girl he had found was like his mother; she did not laugh at his tinkering, but applauded and showed an interest in it. He married her.

He never forgot that little jewelry shop on Baker Street. Every day of my school-age years I could see the Baker Street shop. I didn't have to go far. So deeply did Ford feel it a symbol of his early dream that he had it dismantled and moved to Greenfield Village.

He also reconstructed the old brick barn from Bagley Street, which he always called the birthplace of the Ford car.

The reason they called Ford's early cars Tin Lizzies, he once explained to me, was that you could practically fix one with any old can opener. And there were jokes going around in the old days that Ford made his cars out of old tin cans.

Mr. Ford didn't mind the endless jokes about his early cars as long as people kept buying the cars. "I don't care if they laugh, as long as they've got their hand in their pocket to pull out the money," he would say. His early Fords sold for $850. He always worked at getting the price lower.

He also believed in making a car last as long as possible, and for a time, against the advice and wishes of just about everyone in his company management group, he did the same thing with cars as was later done with rubber tires—he reconditioned them. A person could have practically a new car built out of an old one for a couple of hundred dollars. Most Ford executives took advantage of this offer.

Ford lived to see the day when planned obsolescence became the credo of the whole auto industry, and he disapproved. He really did want to see every family owning a car and all cars lasting for many years. He didn't like putting on airs and buying a new car just because it was new. All through his life Ford never owned a car with exterior custom coach work. He did not foresee the day when car owners would change cars every year, trading in the old model and paying the balance in cash. And he certainly never foresaw that whole companies would be set up to handle installment payments on cars. It was a cash-and-carry world he grew up in, and he did not like men buying things they couldn't pay for immediately. "John, don't ever buy what you can't see your way clear to pay for," he would warn me. "I hope you will remember that."

Thus spoke the Wizard of Dearborn, which incidentally was originally called Dearbornville when it was just a mud-road small settlement about ten miles from Detroit.

It was another man, the Wizard of Menlo Park, to whom Ford gave the highest praise for providing encouragement while he was developing a gasoline-driven car. It was interesting the way fate and Ford's determination finally brought Ford and Thomas Edison together.

After Ford left the farm for the second time in 1891 as a young married man, his first job was with the Edison Illuminating Company, which later became the Detroit Edison Company.

He was working in electricity for the first time, but so mechanical was he that he soon was made chief engineer. He might have used his knowledge to develop an electric car, but something happened that made him interested in internal combustion engines.

Someone wanted him to help repair a European combustion engine, and he was thrilled to see the inner workings of the machine, which operated on a four-cycle principle. It opened his mind. He became busy in his backyard barn figuring out how to work such an engine into a horseless carriage.

By luck he met Edison at a professional meeting. Edison listened to him as best he could, considering that he was very hard of hearing. Ford shouted—which is hard to imagine, since he was soft-spoken unless riled—explaining all about what he was doing to get power for an engine from exploding liquid hydrocarbons in piston-fitted cylinders.

Ford was afraid of two things—that Edison couldn't hear him and that Edison, being an electricity man, would not respect the gas engine. But suddenly Ford got through to him, and Edison's face lighted up as he saw the tremendous thing Ford was trying to do.

Edison got so enthusiastic that he thumped the table he was sitting at as he advised Ford to keep going with his gas engine and not turn to the electric one.

Ford came riding out of his Bagley Street shop in his first car in 1896, and as soon as he could afford it, he wooed the friendship of Edison and almost lived in his shadow. Even with me, his voice took on reverential tones as he talked of how great Edison was and how much his encouragement had influenced his life.

People could not understand why Ford went to infinite trouble and expense, during Edison's lifetime, to dismantle the whole of Menlo Park, where Edison had invented the light bulb, and bring it piecemeal to Greenfield Village. They thought Ford was doing it just to honor Edison's achievement in electricity. But everyone who knew Ford knew he also did it to honor Edison for his help in bringing about the gas-powered car as thought through by Ford.

Before I forget, I want to mention a very important event in my life that involved Thomas Alva Edison. I was six years old in 1929, and Mr. Ford had invited President Hoover to come to Greenfield Village for the dedication of Menlo Park.

I met the President, but what stand out in my mind were other things—such as Edison's ear trumpet, the like of which I'd never seen. Edsel Ford, who was then president of his father's company, presented Mr. Ford with an exact duplicate of that first electric light that Edison had made years before. It had been made from bits and pieces thrown out on the dump at Menlo Park that had been hauled to Greenfield Village in Michigan.

President Hoover did not come away from the ceremony empty-handed. He too received a replica of the first incandescent light.

Ford did not call his first car an automobile, or even a horseless carriage. It was, technically, a "quadricycle," being made for the most part with bicycle parts and a driving engine.

When Ford would tell about his first noisy ride around the neighborhood, he would chuckle as he recalled that everything bad happened to make it a discouraging event. First, the hour of night, 4:00 A.M. Then a spring broke and he had to stop to replace it. And it started to rain, so he got all wet.

And worst of all for his ego, very few people ran to their windows or came out to watch, even though it certainly was noisy enough. But he added that he had received enough publicity afterwards to last a lifetime.

Most people think Ford developed the Model T car without much trouble and very early in the game, but nothing could be further from the truth. A whole procession of cars followed that quadricycle before he developed the Model T. Many problems had to be solved. For example, that first car would not back up or turn around; he would have to get out and lift the back

Mr. Ford, Dad (in fedora), and the captain on the *Oscar II*, Ford's Peace Ship.

This picture of Dad in a Model T racer was taken when he was a test driver at the old Highland Park plant. The car is now in the Henry Ford Museum at Greenfield Village.

A young Henry Ford, already well on his way to becoming the world's most famous industrialist, on vacation with Dad at the Au Sable Trout and Game Club. This is one of my favorite photographs, because it shows Mr. Ford as I knew him—relaxed and informal.

Thomas Edison, one of the many famous people I've had the privilege to meet. Few know that many of Mr. Ford's innovations were really from the brain of Edison. Ford had a brilliant knack for having the right "idea people" around him and using their ideas to their fullest potential.

Henry Ford (second from left), unidentified person, Mother, Will Rogers, Edsel Ford.

Mother loved to dress in period costumes for the many Greenfield Village festivals.

Mrs. Ford was interested in highway beautification long before it became fashionable. Here she is with one of her pet projects: a roadside fruit and vegetable stand for farmers that would be economical as well as profitable. Mother was responsible for the design and construction of this miniaturized display.

Mother in riding outfit, 1942.

Our early Ford Road home,
where I lived as a child.

One of Mr. and Mrs. Ford's sump-
tuous homes, Richmond Hill, under
construction at Ways, Georgia.
Mother and Dad had complete
responsibility for the building of
the entire project.

Fairlane, the Fords' estate in Dearborn.

Clara and Henry Ford with Dad in part of Clara's old-fashioned flower garden at Fairlane. She and Dad worked hard overseeing the maintenance of her many gardens.

Henry Ford as a young man (left); me at about the same age. The resemblance is particularly striking when the eyes and forehead are covered.

Only two of these midget race cars were built. Mr. Ford gave one to his grandson Billy, and one to me. Mine was red with black fenders, and Billy's was all black. Note personalized license plate: JCD 15, my initials and age.

end around. He also had to straighten out his own thinking, because his first concept was to aim for speed in racing cars and thus become famous.

Ironically, though Ford raced and won, it was Barney Oldfield who became the renowned speed driver, thanks to Henry Ford. In fact, they used to kid each other about having made each other famous.

Barney Oldfield, who drove Ford's 999 race car to victory in Los Angeles, New York, and Chicago, used to tell Ford that he had made Ford famous. Ford would come back with the retort that he had made Barney Oldfield famous. Oldfield would have the last word when he would say, "Humph, but I did the better job," because Ford could not deny that his fame and wealth had grown far in excess of that of the noted racer.

I once asked Mr. Ford how the word "automobile" became popular, and he said it had been used by a Frenchman who had invented a car sometime after 1900. The car had been shown in a magazine that Ford bought.

Ford liked to tell the true stories of what happened when he rode around in his first quadricycle. The truth was funnier than the newspaper cartoons that were always appearing. On one occasion Ford was booming along on Woodward Avenue in Detroit, and a cyclist was so overwhelmed by the sight of Ford in his strange contraption that he fell off his bicycle and in front of the wheels of Ford's car. Ford was just as shocked as he was and stopped his car instantly, leaving the man pinned under the front wheels.

Ford jumped off and told the man not to worry and not to move. Then, single-handed, Ford lifted the front of the car while the man rolled out. He would chuckle as he thanked the Lord that the first car was made with bicycle wheels. "I wouldn't have been so lucky today," he once said. "They'd sue me for all I've got." Come to think of it, the danger of lawsuits may have been one reason that Ford usually preferred to be driven and not to get behind the wheel himself.

After the quadricycle, Ford set about designing a car that

would establish speed records. Appropriately enough, it was a champion cyclist named Tom Cooper who befriended Ford and invested his money in the first racer. But it was a very expensive project and required not only Cooper's money but all the money that Ford could scrape together from his job and his farm back home in Dearborn township. The car drew a lot of laughs because it wasn't a low-slung elegant racer like its competitor, the Winton. It was a case of beauty and the beast. And beauty got left behind. With Ford at the wheel, the ugly car crossed the finish line first at the Grosse Point Racing Track on October 1, 1901.

Ford believed in luck, and no wonder. The Long Island train had demolished his chief competitor's racer at a grade crossing. That was Henri Fournier, the odds-on favorite, who had planned to enter a Mors car.

The only sad thing about the victory for Ford was that he had had to sell his first car to help finance the racer. It would be many years before he could find it and bring it back in triumph. It is today on display in the Ford Museum.

I never rode in it, but as a child I did sit in it and listen to Mr. Ford tell his stories about it.

It is said that Ford's old 1896 quadricycle is the car that launched America into modern times. I remember once I was arguing with Mr. Ford about the schooling that he had planned for me and that I considered very old-fashioned. I said, "But, sir, these are different times—this is the modern age and . . ."

He didn't let me finish. "Young man," he exploded, "I invented the modern age!"

And so he did.

The 999 was Ford's most famous racer, and at the Grosse Pointe Racing Track in October 1902, with Barney Oldfield at the wheel, it finished a full half-mile ahead of the closest competitor. Oldfield, incidentally, had been a champion bicycle racer before turning to auto racing.

At this point, cars were still an expensive hobby. The problem was that Henry Ford was concentrating on building cars with speed potential that nobody except race drivers wanted. He was becoming famous for speed, but this didn't line his pockets or feed little Edsel. In other words, commercially Ford was still at ground zero.

But a good thing happened as a result of the publicity that Ford got through racing. A wealthy Detroit coal dealer named Alex Malcomson became interested in investing in Ford's potential, especially since Ford had a new concept, adapted from his watch concept—to make a car so cheap that every family could own one.

This time there was nothing fly-by-night or bargain basement about the project. They set up a more expensive garage and in November 1902 formed Ford and Malcomson, Ltd. By June 1903, with more investors, they had incorporated the Ford Motor Company. The first motor car came out for $100 less than the Olds. It cost $850, and its big advertising line was that it had been made by "the same genius which conceived the world's record maker—the 999." The advertisement further bragged that the Ford car was "The most reliable machine in the world—a two-cylinder car of ample power for the steepest hills and the muddiest roads."

The first sales agent was John Wanamaker, who had the New York territory. Amusingly, Wanamaker assigned his toy-department manager to sell the Ford car, along with other toys. Wanamaker looked at horseless carriages as a fad and was not sure that this adult toy would catch on. But in 1906 he was able to brag that five thousand Ford cars had been sold in one season.

It was not exactly true that Ford's first advertised car could go up a hill easily. Even when he finally got the four-cylinder Model T going, there were still problems with hill climbing, and drivers would write letters to Ford complaining that they would get halfway up the hill and then have to coast back down, turn around, and go up the hill backwards. Somehow the gas was not getting to the motor on a tilt.

And, of course, there was that pesky problem of having to crank the motor by hand to get it started. This prevented almost every female from driving a Ford car. If General Motors had not come up with automatic starters, perhaps the electric runabout, like the Columbia (which was popular in 1904), might have beaten out the gas-driven motor after all. At least a lady could drive it and remain a lady. She didn't have to wrestle a motor to get it started.

On the other hand, she couldn't use it very long without getting it charged.

Most people don't realize that there really were two Model As. They think there was only the Model A that followed the Model T. But the truth is that after Ford's first quadricycle, the first production cars for sale were called Model As, also.

Ford worked his way through the alphabet, picking letters he liked for his succession of early models, and not till he got to T did he have a winner. It was his bonanza.

Only when the Model T's popularity started to fade did Ford turn to designing a new car. As he once mentioned, he didn't want an XYZ. Instead he returned to the A.

The big change from the Model T to the Model A was in the transmission. Also, he got rid of the hand crank, although there was an electric starter available in the last of the Model Ts, if you wanted to pay extra.

The price of the Model T had gone down from $850 to about $475 for a stripped-down version. And if a farmer wanted the chassis only, on wheels, of course—wheels, motor, and hood— he could buy it for $375 or so. Farmers would use it as a power take-off to run a threshing machine or to cut trees for lumber. I have snapshots of a Model T chassis being used as a tractor.

How many Model T Fords are still in existence? The best estimate is 100,000. Many of them are in other countries.

It is still the name that excites the greatest curiosity and admiration. The ugly old Model T was produced from October 1, 1908, to May 31, 1927. In those nineteen years, approximately fifteen and a half million were built. Ford was very proud of it, in spite of the fact that some people suffered broken arms from hanging on to the crank too long when they were starting it. And others dislocated their shoulders.

Henry Ford had no sympathy for them. At our house he would say, "It's their own darn fault. They ought to learn to do it properly."

In my youth there were still plenty of Model Ts around, and I did learn to crank one properly. It was very amusing that Model T owners didn't worry too much about running out of gas, because they could always stop at some farmer's place and borrow some cheap kerosene. It is also amusing, looking back, that to control the speed, gasoline was fed by a hand lever at the steering wheel. The gas tank was under the driver's seat, and a dip stick had to be used to measure gas.

The peak year for the Model T was 1925. It had become mighty fancy—horn, self-starter, flower vases, even foot-fed gas. Ford was spoiling all the fun, and by 1927 it was all over for the Model T.

Ford shut down to retool for a new model.

When Ford unveiled his Model A at Madison Square Garden in New York City, it was a mob scene. As I heard the story, over half a million customers had plunked down money even before they saw the new model in showrooms all over the country, in order to get one of the first models in their towns and cities.

To have a new Model A was class with a capital C.

Ford had a fine contempt for every auto but his own. Mention Oldsmobile, and Ford would sneer a little and launch into his story of how he had had to help the early Olds designer, Malcolm Forrest Loomis, pick up the engine from the street because it kept falling out of the car.

Ransom Eli Olds, who was developing that auto at the turn of the century, was an old friend and competitor of Henry Ford, and Ford was always grateful for one lesson he had learned from what had happened to Olds.

Olds had made a great success of his first car, which was considered inexpensive. But the Olds stockholders insisted—against

Olds's judgment—that he switch to a fancier, more elegant car to appeal to the wealthy person. It was a financial disaster. Because of that, Ford determined that come hell or high water he was going to gain control of his own company and not let any stockholders tell him what to do.

But what actually triggered his move was a suit by two stockholders for a higher distribution of company profits.

No one was going to tell Henry Ford what to do with his money or how to run his business!

People still talk about how much money the early backers of Ford made on a very small investment. It was Ford's third venture that was the moneymaker. He had determined that he would need $100,000 to do the job right when he formed the Ford Motor Company. And that was the authorized capital of the new company. A thousand shares were issued, at $100 a share.

But money was hard to come by when the company came into being—June 16, 1903.

All that Alexander Malcomson was able to talk people out of was $28,000, a far cry from the $100,000 Ford had hoped for.

There were only eleven stockholders besides Ford, who was supplying the car design and the know-how. The story of one is especially interesting—the only woman investor. She was Roselle Couzens, a sister of one of the other investors. She had $200 painstakingly saved up from her job as a schoolteacher. She liked the daring, zany-sounding idea of investing in an automobile, even though everyone said it would never replace the horse, but she agonized over whether it wasn't too risky for her entire savings. She compromised by buying $100 worth of stock with half her savings. Only sixteen years later, when Ford bought out the stockholders, the schoolteacher's return was $260,000. And that didn't include the $95,000 in dividends her stocks had earned.

The way I heard the story, in 1919 it cost Ford something over $100 million to buy out the remaining stockholders of his company and make it a totally family-owned business. John and

Horace Dodge received $12.5 million each based not on money investments but rather on stock they had received in return for $10,000 worth of engines.

Two lawyers who had invested money at Malcomson's insistence—John W. Anderson and Horace H. Rakham—each received $12.5 million on a similar investment, and John S. Gray's estate received $25 million. It is a pity that Gray did not live to see the good thing that had happened to his investment of $10,500. Gray had been the president of the German-American Savings Bank when Malcomson was running around gathering money for Ford. Gray thought it was a very wild and speculative venture he was investing in and did so most reluctantly. To allay his fears about how the company would be run, Ford and Malcomson made him president of the Ford Motor Company.

The irony of the story of the investors is that Malcomson, who had supplied the first money and enthusiasm and had helped set things up as well as twisting the arms of his friends to get them to throw money into the high-risk company, fared the worst.

The story of Malcomson is that he had anted up a guarantee that he would pay all the company's bills up to a limit of $3,000. He also provided the legal work, and Ford and he were to share equally 51 percent of the company's stock.

But the company's research and development bills exceeded the $3,000 limit by several thousand dollars. Malcomson was so nervous about having his reputation and credit rating associated with such a wild-blue-yonder investment that he paid the bills under the name of his bookkeeper, James Couzens.

Malcomson could not see much future in Ford Motor Company and wanted to go back into the coal business. He offered Ford his share of 25.5 percent of the company for $175,000. When Ford paid him off in 1906, Malcomson thought he was very lucky to be out and to have gotten his own price. But had he held on just thirteen years more, he would have been worth $250 million as equal owner with Ford.

The smart one, who received the highest percentage on his investment, was James Couzens, the bookkeeper, who held out when the others settled and as a result received $39.5 million. Couzens had put into the company $900 cash and $1,500 in notes.

Couzens had also had the foresight to buy out another early investor, and that is the saddest story of them all. It involves Albert Strelow, who put $5,000 into the Ford Motor Company as one of the original eleven. Then Strelow went gold prospecting in British Columbia and thought he had struck it rich. He suddenly needed money to develop his mine, and Couzens gave him $25,000.

As it turned out, by 1914 Strelow had lost every penny in his bad gold mine and returned to Detroit broke. Had he hung on to his Ford stock, it would have been worth many millions.

Ford was very proud of the way he had gotten the investors to sell out their stocks in a mini-panic. He did it with three clever moves—two of them rumors and one of them based on truth. The true part was that he made his son president of Ford Motor Company on the last day of the year of 1918. This gave people the impression that he was not as interested in Ford Motor Company as he had been.

Then he let two rumors make the rounds. The first was that he was going to develop another car and then start a new company that would compete with Ford. Specifically, the rumor held that he was going to go into business with his friend Harvey Firestone and manufacture a car that would sell for at least $100 less than the $460 that the Model T cost at that point.

The other rumor—which really rocked his investors back on their heels and made them desperate to sell—was that Ford was secretly planning to sell his own Ford Motor stock to General Motors.

Then, once the stockholders were really nervous, tricky Ford sent secret agents around to offer to buy out the shareholders' stock for $7,500 a share. Everyone but Couzens finally accepted $12,500 a share.

Ford had to borrow $60 million to complete paying the

stockholders off. At the time he was so happy that, according to what I was later told, he hopped around the room and danced a jig when he heard that he was now the sole owner of Ford Motor Company. But hard times were around the corner, and the banks were tough about not extending his payment time. Some said the New York bankers were licking their chops and ready to send men to put Ford plants into receivership.

But Ford had one more ace up his sleeve. He suddenly sent huge shipments of cars to all his dealerships, forcing them to make bank loans and pay him in cash. Fords were so much in demand that the dealers had no choice, and the practice of loading up dealerships with cars and parts began.

Ford made all kinds of business history. He had organized his company in 1903, and in twenty-three years, based on that initial cash capital of $28,000 of other people's money, he had earned profits of over $900 million dollars.

Not only did Ford hire former criminals in fairly large numbers and rehabilitate them, but his was one of the first large companies to hire the handicapped, including the blind.

You could say that in his automobile development and expansion, Ford went through all the stages of education. Bagley was kindergarten, Piquette was grade school, Highland Park was high school, and Rouge was the great university.

Now and then, over a drink at the Dearborn Country Club, people who knew of my family's Ford connection used to get to talking about Ford's early cars, and there was always a dispute over the year in which Ford came crashing out of that wall on Bagley Street. Some books claim the year was 1893, and others say 1896. It's of no consequence today, except as a matter of curiosity and of setting the record straight.

The problem back in those days was that a man named George B. Selden claimed to have the earliest patent for an automobile and was making all the car builders pay for the use of his patent. Ford refused to pay and was taken to court.

Selden filed suit in October 1903. Ford's defense was that he had constructed his quadricycle before Selden received his patent in 1895. Everyone in the trade was calling Ford a David fighting a Goliath.

The ironic thing is that Selden had never built the horseless carriage that he had patented.

As it turned out, the case was not settled on the basis of the date of invention that either Ford or Selden was claiming. Ford finally won because Selden's lawsuit was based on a two-cycle engine and Ford had developed a four-cycle engine, which was, the court decided, an altogether different thing.

It is hard to comprehend today the impact that Ford's winning the suit made on the industry. Because of "David," manufacturers were freed from the tributes levied by Goliath.

Sometimes things happened that made Ford more determined than ever to be completely independent and self-contained. His break with an aluminum company is a prime example. The aluminum company was a monopoly—a ruthless one, Ford claimed. It insisted that Ford sell back all his scrap metal for peanuts. Ford was furious. He had been selling the scrap to cookware companies to be made into pots and pans.

The president of the aluminum company got on his high horse. Ford sent a man to talk with him, and he came back reporting that the president had said Ford could "bloody well take it or leave it."

Ford fretted and fumed, but not for long. He quickly shifted over to steel and ordered his plant to retool. When Henry Ford got angry, cost was no object. In the long run, it was a good move, because steel was stronger.

Ford got more and more excited over the potential of steel. He was going to mass-produce a plane by stamping it out of stainless steel. But the Depression came along, and his plans for a plane in every garage were put on the back burner.

How many early cars did Ford manufacture, and how cheap did they eventually get?

In 1910, the first full production year, Ford turned out 10,607 cars. By 1913 he was producing 200,000 cars, half of all the cars sold. The next year, 1914, saw one car coming off the assembly line every forty seconds.

The twenty-millionth car came off the line to great fanfare in 1931, and there are many pictures of Ford and Edsel looking at it. It was a Model A.

The forty-millionth came off the line twenty-two years later, in 1953.

As for price, the lowest a Ford ever got was in December 1924, when the Model T's price came down to $290, a long way from $850 in 1909. Ford's efficiency and standardization of parts had done the trick, as had the lack of such frills as fancy paint jobs.

Some people believe that Ford never used anything but black, giving rise to the joke that you could have any color Ford as long as it was black. The truth is that Ford originally supplied three colors—a dullish color called Brewster green, a dull gray, and black.

It turned out that the black paint dried fastest, so to keep up with orders they slapped black on everything.

It's hard to realize how fiercely proud Henry Ford was of his early cars and how reluctant he was to change them. He held off until sales had gone way down and other designers were threatening to get ahead of him.

The best illustration of this was what happened to Mother's old boss, C. H. Wills, who took it upon himself, behind Ford's back, to prepare a new and better design as a surprise. Mother said it was a super-looking thing.

But evidently Ford took one look and went berserk. He seized a sledge hammer and started knocking the thing apart. He kept banging away until he had pretty well demolished it. For some time after that, no one tried to surprise Ford with improvements he hadn't ordered himself.

Ford had quite a time telling designers what he wanted. The truth is he was not too sharp on blueprints. Car blueprints are especially complicated because of the small scale. So he had a large blackboard on which his designers and engineers would draw the car and discuss it with him tactfully, explaining what everything meant.

Because he hadn't their education, he was sometimes embarrassed at not knowing data or the terminology used. For that reason, he was determined that I should have a good education, including mechanical drawing.

Thanks to Ford, I had an automated childhood. Practically before I walked, I had a pedal race car. And as soon as I could handle it, a small car with a motor was made for me. At that time no American car engine was small enough, so Henry Ford put in a small imported engine.

Then I had a Red Bug, an electric play car. And when I was seven, Ford gave me a 23 Indy race car, Fronty Ford.

I had cars almost too numerous to mention. The number would have to have been in the dozens—maybe two dozen—before I was out of school. I had a number of Model Ts, a number of Model As, an MG, a Bugatti, and a Citroën.

When I was graduated from Deerfield Academy, I got a Continental. I was not happy. I had wanted a custom Continental, and all I got was an ordinary Continental.

I was always redesigning cars a bit to suit my fancy, and of course the Ford experts did the work. When I was given a '41 Mercury convertible, I got the idea of taking the running boards off. It struck me that running boards were dumb. Eventually running boards did come off all cars, in the interest of streamlining.

The Red Bug and the MG wound up in the Ford Museum, but there is nothing to show that they were ever mine.

After I had driven some of my cars awhile and become tired of them, they would go to Edsel Ford's house for his children. Sometimes Edsel Ford would test a car for a little while, and it would finally be given to me.

Almost all my cars were slightly custom built. At the very least I would want special leather interiors and special paint jobs.

When I was a little kid playing with the Henry Ford grand-children, much of our conversation was about our cars.

Many of the toys I had were duplicates of what they had. They had a Red Bug; I had a Red Bug. Billy had a midget race car which could be driven on the street, same as mine. I always had special license plates with my initials on them, 'way back when such things were not easy to get. You could get your initials only if you knew somebody.

I still have the license plate I had in 1938, when I was fifteen years old. It says JCD 15. As I tooled along, everyone who knew me recognized what my license plate stood for: "John Côté Dahlinger, age 15."

9
The Men Around Ford

There were many men around Henry Ford as far back as I can remember, competing with one another to be most important to him. Of course, every one of them thought—or talked as if he thought—that *he* was the most important. Only Ford knew who was important, and he played it close to the chest.

He had a terrible way, I thought, of setting men against each other and making them ever more competitive. He would make them distrust each other by saying such things as, "So-and-so is no friend of yours."

Ford managed to get Dad into just such a disagreeable situation. I would hear him say, "Ray, Harry Bennett is no friend of yours." And I'm sure he must have told Bennett, "You know, Harry, Ray Dahlinger is no friend of yours."

It had come to the point where Dad and Harry were forever trying to top each other. If Harry Bennett had a big party for all the Ford executives at his estate, Ray Dahlinger had an even bigger party at our estate, with horses for anyone who wanted to ride and harness racing for those who wanted to watch, and enough steak to feed a Detroit hunger march.

The two men's functions were quite similar. Each was a Ford confidant. Each drove Henry Ford around whenever he wanted. Each spied on the other executives for him.

And I do believe each would have laid down his life for Henry Ford.

But they certainly wouldn't have laid down their lives for each other. Neither man had a title that accurately explained what he did for Henry Ford. Dad's was manager of the Ford Farms, but he could be doing something totally unrelated to the Farms. Harry Bennett was head of security for Ford. He carried a gun.

But for that matter, Dad carried a gun. Mother carried a gun. Ford carried a gun. My driver carried a gun. Ford's driver carried a gun.

Looking back, it seems like some kid's game of cowboys and Indians, only they took their game seriously. Everyone wanted to be a cowboy, and only Indians were targets.

Why did everyone carry a gun? Part of it was that they liked the Wild West tradition. And part of it was that they really did feel that they were living in troubled times, with violence possible at any time: they worried about union troubles, personal safety, and just the fact that everyone carried a lot of money.

Both Bennett and Dad practiced target religiously—but not together. There was a shooting gallery in the room in back of Dad's office and another one at Rouge that Bennett used.

Bennett was one of the best shots I have ever seen. I'll tell you how good he was. One day someone came into his office whom he didn't like—and in Henry Ford's day the executives were all permitted to let all their hates hang out. The man said something that gave Bennett an excuse to say something nasty in return. Bennett then added that the man had better take the cigar out of his mouth. Much annoyed, the fellow said, "You'd better make me." Bennett whipped the gun out of his pocket and shot the cigar out of the fellow's mouth as the man turned away from him, fortunately presenting a profile.

I don't believe Dad was ever able to, or wanted to, top that. Nor would he have wanted to top Bennett's prize possessions— some lions and tigers that he kept in a building near his home. I didn't know about them at the time and didn't hear about them until later, although I was a guest at Bennett's home many times.

One of the stories making the rounds was that Bennett tried to give one of his lions to another Ford man, and it ended up at the police station after it escaped from its new owner and roamed the neighborhood. The story goes that Bennett, being a big shot of the Ford Motor Company, was not even reprimanded by the police.

But Dad topped Bennett in the most important way—Dad was closer to Henry Ford in a personal way than Bennett could ever hope to be. Bennett worked his way up to be the absolute power at the Rouge, whereas Dad had long been the absolute power of Dearborn and the Farms, as well as having been a personal friend of Ford's for a much longer period of time.

Since his fame made him a target for all eyes and kept him from enjoying himself in public in a relaxed way, Mr. Ford preferred to stay in the background and let people come to him. Part of his mental recreation was listening to the men squeal about what the others were doing.

Largely because of the way he pitted one man against the other, Ford had very few close friends.

For a time, Dad and Bill Stout were a set of warring gladiators, to Ford's amusement.

William Stout, the man credited with designing the Ford trimotor airplane, was egocentric. As was frequently said at our house, he thought he was "the greatest thing since sliced bread."

Ford had made him head of aircraft design, but it was said

that Stout stole the design of the Ford trimotor from Tony Fokker. Tony Fokker himself said so.

Stout maintained that he already had a wing design and after seeing the Fokker merely enlarged upon it and added the corrugated metal. To his dying day, Dad claimed that Stout had stolen the design, and that other than making the plane out of metal there was very little difference between his plane and Fokker's.

Stout resented my father's access to Ford. Dad had the Boss's ear. Stout was not a pilot at that time, and Dad was. Some of the senior test pilots felt they knew as much as Stout because of their actual experiences.

Dad and some of the others in the group known as the "back door gang" were responsible for building the Ford 14A, the biggest American plane of its time. But it never got off the ground. It had one problem—they were never able to produce engines powerful enough for practical flight.

There was always a mini-war or two going on in the upper echelons of the Ford Company—egged on by Ford. The battles would make good gossip grist, not only for the way the men would undercut each other but for the way Henry Ford would refuse to come to grips with a situation. In fact, I would say Mr. Ford enjoyed the little power wars as much as those who were on the sidelines did—that is, until it got too hot and there was a showdown.

One of the power wars involved Bill Knudsen and Charlie Sorensen. Actually they were more or less duplicates of each other, inasmuch as they were both production men. Basically they did the same things, and it was a case of who did them best. With the two of them trying to outdo each other, Mr. Ford had the best of two worlds.

It was Knudsen who finally went to Ford and said, "You have to make a choice between me and Sorensen."

Ford, as usual, didn't want to make a choice and kept procrastinating; consequently Bill Knudsen left the company. He wasn't really fired; he could have stayed. Mr. Ford would have liked to continue this Sorensen-Knudsen affair, having the services of two of the best production men in the country.

I would say Knudsen was the winner, because he went to General Motors and became its president.

Sorensen was supposed to become president of Ford Motor Company, but just at his moment of triumph he was fired instead. I'll tell you about that situation in a moment.

The nicest thing you could say about Sorensen was that he never held a grudge. He was head of production, and he was like a machine himself, almost without nerves and just a work machine. I don't believe he ever came to any of our big parties for the Ford gang.

Sorensen had his own peculiar way of firing people. He would simply hire another man to do the same job, and suddenly, when the first man came to work, there was nothing left for him to do. Usually, the man's pride would dictate that he quit rather than stand around and watch the new man work.

Sorensen and Edsel got along well, working as a team to keep the cars flowing smoothly off the assembly line. People around the plant said that Sorensen was just like Henry Ford in a way: neither cared what you thought of him as long as you got the job done—that you could call either a son of a bitch and he would just laugh it off or ignore it if you were doing your job.

Sorensen even laughed it off when Bennett told him on several occasions that he was fired. He just acted as if it never happened. Nor did he complain to the real boss, Henry Ford. He just acted stoic or amused and went on about his business.

In 1943, after Edsel died, there was some question whether Sorensen would be president of Ford or whether Henry Ford would take over the helm again. Ford had led Sorensen to believe that he was next up. But strange forces were at work. The inside story was that the Edsel family was afraid that if a strong man like Sorensen took over, it would keep Henry II, the grandson, in a minor position for years to come. The story was that Clara Ford joined a conspiracy and passed the word to Henry Ford's secretary, Frank Campsall, that it would be a kindness to Henry Ford and avoid embarrassment if Sorensen would just leave on his own.

He left, and the petty postscript to the story is that someone at the plant wired Sorensen to be sure to return the company car he was driving.

Harry Bennett was a short, stocky, squared-off man. He had been an amateur fighter in the navy. He always reminded me of a bantam rooster. He was tough-talking, and with a few drinks he wanted to fight.

Now and then I would hear that he had taken a poke at somebody in the company. Edsel could hardly stand him, but he made an effort to be civil because his father enjoyed Bennett and relied on him a lot. Edsel never made waves where his father was concerned.

To show how Bennett operated, consider how Frank Kulick was treated, after he had practically lost his life for the honor of the Ford Motor Company. He was in an auto race at the Michigan state fair, riding for Ford, of course, when one of the tires exploded and a piece of heavy rubber hit him in the head. Unable to control the six-cylinder racer, Kulick crashed into a fence and was rushed to a hospital.

Ford, who witnessed the accident, was very upset and vowed that he was through racing. "I'll never let any of my men risk their lives this way again," he said and gave Kulick reason to believe his job at Ford was secure forever.

But Ford and Bennett later became disenchanted with Kulick for some reason, and Bennett said he would get rid of him. He certainly did. Bennett asked Kulick to lie down on the running board of his car and listen to the motor to see what was wrong with it while Bennett drove it a short distance.

Kulick agreed, but Bennett, instead of test-driving the car slowly, went speeding out of the plant grounds. He then spun around so quickly that Kulick could not hang on and fell off the running board. Without stopping to see if Kulick was hurt, Bennett raced back through the plant gates and gave orders to the guards to "keep that son of a bitch out of here."

The way I heard the story over and over again—it was a classic—Kulick was not even permitted back into the plant to pick up his belongings. I believe they were sent out to him at the gate. What his high crime had been I don't recall, but I have a feeling it was something trivial.

Somewhere along the line Dad's friendly competition with Harry Bennett became a full-scale war. Henry Ford had become old and senile, and Bennett used this fact to his own advantage, becoming in effect the czar of the Rouge plant. The difference between the two men was that Mr. D. protected Ford and never tried to take over. Dad was satisfied with all the jobs Ford gave him, but Bennett was never satisfied. No matter how much power he had, he always aimed for a little more.

It was said around the plant that Bennett had a goon squad of several thousand men ready for any violence. He called them security men, but many were thugs, ex-boxers and ex-convicts. He himself had started simply as Ford's bodyguard and had built the security branch of Ford Motor Company into a big operation under the pretext of fighting the unions.

The word around Rouge was that Bennett had gotten swelled out of proportion—the head was getting a little too large for the body. Not content with being the bull of the Rouge, he sent a man over to Dearborn, Dad's territory, to learn how Mr. D. did things.

It was Mother who realized what was going on and told Dad that the new man who was ferreting out Mr. D.'s little ways had to be one of Bennett's boys. "He's after your job, Ray," she said. "Can't you see it? Bennett is grooming him to take over from you."

Once Mother mentioned it, it all became clear to Dad, and he asked Ford about it. Sure enough, Ford admitted that Bennett was suggesting that the other man could do Ray Dahlinger's job. In this case Ford acted firmly, immediately firing the other man and telling Bennett that no one was going to take over Mr. D.'s job as long as he, Ford, was around.

Bennett, in turn, was dismissed by Henry II. So it came to pass, in Ford's last years, that Dad became his main confidant and spent almost every day with him.

Henry Ford was a man of many moods, sometimes full of gratitude to someone who helped him a great deal, and sometimes not.

The only person Ford ever kept on whom he didn't like was, to my knowledge, Ernest Liebold, who was called many things, including Ford's business secretary, Ford's general secretary, and the general manager of Dearborn Publishing Company.

Liebold seemed to have some strange hold over Mr. Ford, or so my parents thought. Could it have been that Liebold knew too much about the millions of dollars in cash Ford had hidden away, or about the disbursement of Ford's money? Did it have to do with unorthodox methods of doing business? We never found out exactly, but the folks would speculate.

Late in the '30s, when Ford was trying to freeze Liebold out of the company, Dad wrote a letter to Mother, who was away on a trip, about the situation. He wrote:

. . . They are putting the clamps on Liebold, now. Boss told me to tell him not to do anything or have anything to do with the Ford Motor Company. You know he draws a big salary from the Ford Motor Company. Well, I told him and he said, "Did the boss tell you to tell me that?" I said you have nothing to do with Ford Motor Company and don't put in any more raises for the men. He was very sore and mad, he was going to see the boss. Well, the boss talked to him today and I guess told him a plenty.

Boss told me to go after all of them. He said I was the only one that takes interest in the company. He asked about you and said gee, I wish Mrs. D. was here. The three of us would clean house . . .

Ray
(signed)

He meant get rid of the dead weight in the company. Ford was always talking about "cleaning house" and getting rid of Edsel's men. But he hated to do the "getting rid" by himself. He'd sic one man on another.

He sicced everyone on Liebold, including Dad, but still Liebold hung on. Liebold had made a lot of enemies in the press for riding roughshod over them when they tried to get a story. He was known around the plant as a real Prussian type, and it was he who had arranged for Ford's acceptance of the Nazi decoration. There was even some question about whether Ford knew the decoration was coming before it arrived.

At any rate, Ford eventually did get rid of Liebold; Frank Campsall took his place.

Henry Ford could never have made it in today's industrial world. He had to be absolute boss and own the minds as well as the time of his employees. They had to be, as he put it, "100 per cent Ford Company or I don't want them." As he interpreted this, it meant that if a man bought some stock in another company—and they weren't permitted to buy Ford stock—it would be a treasonous act of disloyalty.

This led to a confrontation between Ford and a man named Klingensmith, who bought not just one stock, but, it was reliably reported to Ford, quite a few stocks. Henry Ford told him, with righteous indignation, that he would just have to get rid of his stock.

"Yes," said Klingensmith, according to Mother, "either that or get rid of Ford Motor Company. I guess I'll get rid of Ford Motor Company." And he walked out. Klingensmith was only one of several executives who decided they couldn't put up with a boss who told them what to do with their money "or else."

On the other hand, Ford could be infinitely kind to the families of his men. He built a hospital for them. He was paternalistic in every way.

Ford had the notion—and he may have been right—that you could train a man in almost any profession you wanted, if you just gave him a chance. The prime example was that of John Wandersee, and men around the plant never ceased marveling and laughing about what Ford did for him.

The story was that Wandersee had been the handyman and errand boy around Ford's workshop in 1902. At a certain point in the experiments, Ford realized he needed a chemist to study chemical reactions on metals and such things as the best kind of paint to use on auto bodies. His eye fell on Wandersee, who was sweeping out the place, and he told the group of men who were around him at the moment, "There is my chemist."

Ford sent the startled handyman out to find out whatever he needed to know. In this case Ford was right, and John Wandersee became the company's head chemist and metallurgist.

Other times, when Mr. Ford guessed wrong and the man could not do what Ford suddenly assigned him, Ford refused to give up and put the man back in his old job. No indeed. Mr. Ford believed that a man should have a dozen chances to prove what he could do before the company gave up on him.

This was especially true for kids who had gone to school at Ford's Village schools. When they came to work at the plant, they would be shuffled around until they were placed in something they could do and do well, and Ford would be proud that his theory had worked.

Henry Ford did the same thing with C. Harold Wills, Mother's old boss, who was a car designer. He sent Wills to study various metals and was rewarded when Wills discovered that molybdenum could be used to make steel lighter and tougher. Wills also designed the Ford logo, which is still used.

Wills, who went by his initials C. H., hated his first name which was Childe. Wills had picked Mother out of the stenographic pool because she was pretty and talented and had caught his eye.

I should explain that, based on the thirty-five-year anniversary watch given her in 1945, Mother must have first gone to work for Ford in 1910. When Wills pulled her out of the steno pool, she had risen to the top position.

Actually, Mother grew up knowing shorthand—at one point her father, who was a professor at Detroit Business University, wrote a book on his own shorthand method, the Côté method. There was the Gregg method, the Pittman, and the Côté.

Returning to Wills, he basically had one of the best deals in the company. He was possibly the only one who received a percentage of profits; this was because he had designed the early engines.

Even so, Ford did not give him the title of designer. Everyone knew what he did, but if titles were used around the Ford plant, they were more a smoke screen than anything else.

Wills did the unforgivable. He eventually left to bring out his own car, using all the money he had earned at Ford.

His savings were considerable. Mother said he had earned as much as $80,000 a year. From all I heard, Wills was quite a hot dog, a dapper Dan, a ladies' man. He always carried a great deal of money on him and was quite flashy with his jewelry, favoring diamond rings and stick pins.

My understanding was that when he left he had over $20 million to start his own automobile company. Unfortunately, he had forgotten the big lesson he had learned at Ford, which was to keep a car within the reach of the average man.

Wills tried to build the ultimate car. It was a wonderful car, but it was very, very expensive. It was built in St. Clair, Michigan, up near Port Huron, and called the Wills–St. Clair. It was a beauty in its day, but Wills didn't last long in the business, because at this time Ford was turning out the $700 Model Ts and Wills was turning out $2,500 luxury cars.

After Wills's company went broke, he showed up at Ford wanting a job again, and Henry Ford refused to see him. He had deserted Ford, and that was that. Mother was pleased that Wills did manage to get a good job with another auto firm.

As I recall, he went to work for Dodge or Chrysler, and I

believe he worked there until he died, sometime after World War II.

Ford was frequently disappointed in the men around him. He explained that in his early days he had been bitterly disappointed in the Dodge brothers, Horace and John, who had been among the original eleven outside stockholders of the Ford Motor Company. They had dared to sue him.

Though they had invested only a few thousand dollars (in trade—motors—not even cash), they had taken him to court, suing for a large share of profit. Ford had told the court that the prime purpose of a business corporation was to employ men at the highest wage possible and to reduce the cost of the goods to the point where the greatest number of people could buy them.

The court disagreed, saying that "a business corporation is carried on primarily for the profit of the stockholders."

After that, when Ford bought full control of his company, he still tried to live by his credo that the major purpose of his company was to make the Ford cheap enough to be within the grasp of every poor farmer and bricklayer.

He smiled grimly as the Dodge brothers became multimillionaires from the company they had built up with Ford money.

Charles Lindbergh was one of Henry Ford's special pets. He identified with Lindbergh, because he felt they both were always being misunderstood by the government and an ungrateful public. Lindbergh had been given the same decoration from Nazi Germany that Ford had, and both were harassed by the press about it. When Lindbergh could not get a job during World War II because his loyalty was in question, Henry Ford gave him a good job in quality control of planes, and would invite him to dinner at his home now and then.

But even before this, Lindbergh would send friendly letters to Ford, applauding something Henry Ford had said. Once he arranged for the Village to get something, and Ford, in turn, sent him a car.

It's a good thing that nepotism was not frowned upon in the

old days as it is today, or the whole Ford gang would have been in trouble. My mother arranged for two of her brothers to receive Ford dealerships. Mother and Dad both worked for Ford, and for a while so did I.

Edsel Ford's wife got her brother-in-law, Ernest Kanzler, on the payroll and helped keep him there even while Henry and some of his cronies tore their hair trying to think of ways to get him out.

Many men got their sons, daughters, brothers, sisters, and fathers a place on the Ford payroll.

Dad also had a brother who had a dealership.

Outside the plant Ford had few friends—especially in later years. Very precious to Ford was his memory of friendship with three important men—John Burroughs, Thomas A. Edison, and Harvey S. Firestone. Ford would speak with great nostalgia about the way the foursome had gone camping together for several weeks every year.

They were not exactly roughing it, as Ford told it, because they were followed by a chuck wagon–type truck, filled with steaks and all the good things. But they would cook the steaks over a fire they made themselves.

As a matter of fact, I was much impressed with the way they made their steaks under the direction of Burroughs, who seemed to be the leader. I still remember how to make these "J.B. steaks":

Cut fresh green branches to spear the steak, so that they will not burn over the fire. Spear a steak, a slice or two of bacon, and a couple of whole onions on the green branch, and hold it over the fire, turning often.

That's all there was to it, but evidently that was the best steak Ford ever had. Burroughs was the only "poor" member of this quartet, and so whenever Ford visited him, he would always take along some steaks as a little present.

But that was not the only present Ford gave Burroughs. Once, he helped him out of a tight financial squeeze.

As Mother told it, Burroughs was in danger of losing his homestead, and Ford simply took care of the mortgage, paying it off. Another time he sent Ford workers to clear the brush. Ford missed the quartet in later years, and though he would go walking many miles with Mother and sometimes with Frank Campsall, he always spoke nostalgically of the camping days.

Each of the three men filled a separate need in Ford. With Firestone, he talked of the future of business and automobiles; they had similar business problems.

Edison was, in a way, the encouraging father figure Ford's own father had failed to be. Mr. Ford almost worshipped Edison for having pounded the table with enthusiasm, urging him to go full speed ahead in the development of his first power-driven vehicle, the quadricycle.

Burroughs took the place of an old hermit who had inspired Ford's childhood interest in nature. Ford was inspired by Burroughs to conserve nature and animal life. As a memorial to Burroughs, Ford had a bird sanctuary built in a portion of his yard at Fairlane that he called Burroughs Nook. I seem to recall there was a heated birdbath and a little statue of Burroughs there as well.

The love and trust Ford could not place in the men around him, he placed in birds.

10
Life Around
the Plant

Mr. Ford never had a female secretary. He always had a male secretary, and I believe this tradition is still being carried on by his grandson.

Henry Ford did not have a way with words, so he did not dictate. I can still see him deciding that a certain letter must be written. He would tell his secretary, Frank Campsall, something like, "You tell those sons of bitches the wheels fall off," and then Campsall would send a very nice letter explaining in elegant language what Mr. Ford had found wrong and what he would like done.

Frank Campsall became Henry Ford's secretary in the late '30s, when Liebold fell from grace. So close to the Fords did Frank Campsall become that he even went along to Georgia or Florida with them in the winter. When he died in 1946, it was at Ford's Georgia estate, Richmond Hill.

Mother and Frank had an easygoing, fun-filled relationship,

and they would write each other long letters whenever Frank was in Georgia.

Since Ford would never write a letter himself and would at most send a telegram, anything Ford wanted Mother to know would come through Campsall.

Frank would sign himself "Grapefruit Frank" because of all the citrus he had to eat down there. He started it the first time by calling himself "Grapefruit Blossom" and, I believe, sending her some blossoms or flowers of some sort. Anyway, her letters to him provide insight into both their relationship and the flow of events at Ford's beloved Greenfield Village, which Mother was looking after in Ford's absence.

Incidentally, I hope it is not lost on the reader that the way for Mother to get a long letter to Henry Ford was to send it to Frank Campsall instead. I'm sure that Ford read all the letters.

Dear Frank:

Well, we've heard of people called the name of a flower before, but it wasn't "Grapefruit Blossom," the name you signed to your letter; however, a rose by any other name would be just as sweet. So O.K. and the blossom was very nice and it did smell grand.

The trees are moving into the village fast and furious and it's starting to look real nice. There are five maples at the Edison house now and you know it looks like they had been there always. You know there's something real homey looking about that old place, sort of a mellow and lived-in look. The McGuffey house is being set up O.K. and it is starting to take on a look of having always been in just that setting—with that very severe and substantial old Lincoln Court-house, it seems as though you just naturally expect to see a log cabin in the offing. You know what we mean, Lincoln, log cabins, books, education, McGuffey—don't they kind of all seem to belong together? Took some pictures, thought the boss might enjoy looking at them.

The Deeds and Abstracts have been signed over to the Ford Motor for Airport Drive and it can be closed about July or no later than August. Smith of the Good Roads told Ray. Also they are going to take down the church at the corner of Southfield and

Joy Road known a long time ago as the Wm. Ford Church. Smith wants to know if the boss wants the brick for any reason.

You know things have been going so fast and furious one can hardly realize that just a little over a week has gone since you left. You know the day after you left Mr. Edsel met Ray and said, "Well, Ray, have you relaxed yet?" and Ray said "You know, Mr. Edsel, last night I made up my mind that I would sleep this morning till I woke up even if it was 11 o'clock—well, I woke at 6 and was over at the plant by 7:30." Mr. Edsel roared.

By the time you get this letter Wilson and Eddie will have arrived, sent everything you asked for in your letter. Sure stepped on it to get out that car, hope it was what the boss wanted. Am enclosing a report on the "44" job you can read to the boss.

Do you know it's been between eight above and five below zero most of the time since you left, and you're writing us telling us you're down there in your shirt sleeves. Didn't your mother ever teach you it isn't nice to gloat over ones less fortunate than you are?? Shame!

(signed)

Henry Ford never refused a friendly offer of antique bricks, so I am sure he wanted them. But anyway, a letter came back by return mail in Frank's straight up-and-down handwriting with all kinds of comments relayed from the Boss and ending with:

Well this will do for today—and leaving all joking aside I'm lonesome for all of you.

The weather has been great with a couple of rainy days.

Yours,
"Grapefruit Frank"

Ford was a great walker, and in one letter Frank tells how they had just come back from a three-mile hike.

There is another letter Campsall sent from Richmond Hill which shows another way Henry Ford kept in such fine physical shape even late in his life. It is dated March 13, 1936, when Ford was seventy-three, and, incidentally, refers to Mother by Ford's pet name for her but spelled "Billie":

The boss and I have a log which I hack at and he cuts every morning between 7:30 and 8. Breakfast is generally about 8. The boss and I—missus about 9—lunch at 1 or 1:30, dinner at 6:30. In between Mrs. reads a lot and has also done considerable with the architect on the new house—which Billie has started to stake out for a final O.K. When I believe they will start working.

The following letter from Mother to Campsall is my favorite for many reasons—including the comments on osteopaths and chiropractors and the playful opening to the letter, which I am sure was aimed more at Henry Ford than at Frank. She had not yet heard from Ford after he had gone to Georgia. And again there was interesting news about the Village (H.F.H. refers to Henry Ford Hospital):

Dear Frank:

We were going to write last night, then when you said on the phone you had sent a letter, waited till today, but none came—you're not fooling us are you, encouraging us then casting us aside. We've heard of these "play-boys" who go South in the winter and to Europe in the summer, we've been cautioned by our parents "not to take any stock in 'em," but somehow we thought YOU were "DIFFERENT." Ah! me, cruel world, we live and learn.

It was great to hear your voice last night, and gee, the boss sounded so natural, Ray bubbled all over for himself, and, well, I was tickled myself I'll admit. Of course, as soon as you hung up there was a *hundred* things we could think of we forgot to tell you, well, seven anyway. First of all wanted to tell you about the little girl Helen, the one with the poor eyesight the boss told me about, he will remember.

It seems it wasn't the doctors at our hospital that had given her up, it was at U of M and so the ones here at H.F.H. are going to give her a try. It seems Mr. Lovett was misinformed about her going blind, that doesn't seem to be the case. It seems her eyesight is bad, but that careful exercise, of the eyes, will tend to bring it back and not let it get any worse. Also, Dr. Coulter found her very constipated, terribly so he said, and he would want to treat her for that before much could be done about her eyes.

I spoke to Mr. Lovett about her and he didn't seem to want to tell me much but Dr. Johnston—the children's doctor at the hospital—says he is going to try and fix up her diet, which is a bit hard because they are Seventh Day Adventists.

Dr. Kreutz, the eye man, is going to treat her eyes. Dr. Coulter would rather not interfere with them. You know how it is, an Osteopath is like a red flag to a bull to those M.D.'s. The first time I talked to Dr. Johnston about Helen he promptly told me, "She's been treating with some Chiropractor." It was so funny, poor Dr. Coulter had treated her *once*. You'd think he was the cause of all her trouble.

Well, Mr. Lovett evidentally thinks it best to give the H.F.H. doctors a trial I guess, and anyway we can always have Dr. Coulter take up where they left off if they don't make a go of it.

Are enclosing some more pictures of the McGuffey house, it shows the opening the boss asked about. The other log has to be cut too, that isn't shown cut. It seems at times a man would wander in and chop wood or other chores for a night's lodging and that is where he slept and reached this "crows nest" by a stair that ran parallel to the side wall.

Isn't that too bad about Mrs. Ford. Wish she could feel a bit better anyway. Called Dr. Sladen last night as the boss said to do. Dr. says he didn't give Mrs. Ford much to do while away, thinking she wouldn't want to be bothered with medicines and such but said he had sent on instructions and medicines by air mail, which of course you know about by now anyway.

Say Frank, just happened to think, wonder if Mrs. Ford would like a hospital bed down there, you know they can be cranked up and if she has to be resting lots of the time, perhaps it would be more comfortable, you know they make a grand rest for the back and knees. We could put it on the truck when it goes down. Think I'll send one of those pillows in any event. They are nice for reading when half lying down.

Shipped the turkey and more cottage cheese today. Everything is O.K. at the residence. Fixed the leak on the front porch where it rained in so badly. Mrs. Ford ought to be glad to hear that.

Don't bother her about those paint samples,—hope to God, or somebody helps us out but we've gone ahead anyway without them.

We must be getting some of the "unusual weather" you've been having, only it isn't "unusual" here. It started in day before yesterday, rainy and damp—of course any one knows it's damp when it's rainy, let that one pass—and foggy. Right now we can't see beyond the kitchen door. If that is the best you can send us, you can keep it.

We can't think of another thing to say. Oh, almost forgot, the new teacher for the high school seems to be doing O.K. The children say they like him. One girl told me she didn't have time to read two or three story books a week in school as she did before. But now she's learning more. I said I thought that's what they were supposed to go to school for—to learn—and she laughed and said she knew it.

Say, if we don't close this soon you'll be coming home in self-defense, so goodbye, good luck and "take keer o' yerself."

(signed)

When I read articles these days about how executives of big corporations meet the wife of a potential executive before hiring him, I laugh and think of Ford. He was 'way ahead of them. Even before I was born, he had set up a division of the company called the sociology department, in order to find out everything about the wife and her relations with her husband, the prospective employee.

There were many stories going around about how Ford had been a very stuffy, righteous man in his early days of success—before my birth—and had tried to police everyone's morals. He had meddled in the marital lives of his own relatives and even those of his employees.

There was one case, on his wife's side, where, I was told, he had insisted that an estranged husband and wife get back together, and they did—but miserably. In another case, he tried to get a couple back together even though one of them had already remarried.

He held the Catholic view that only the first marriage was

sacred. Of course this was before my time, and I would say that Mr. Ford certainly changed a lot. He no longer thought that all marriages were made in heaven, and his own conduct was a little lax, to say the least.

But to the end Henry Ford believed that even though people were not happy together, it was their duty to keep up appearances and stay together as man and wife.

When the Ford Motor Company started its five-dollars-a-day pay policy, workers were thrilled, but their private lives were placed under even greater scrutiny. It was in the Ford working agreement that one had to live an exemplary life. Some men had to produce marriage certificates, if it was thought they were living in sin. If the suspicion was confirmed and no marriage license appeared, the man quickly disappeared from the plant.

There was also an Americanization program at Ford to teach foreigners the American way of life. Held up as the shining example for all his classmates was the foreign immigrant who memorized the whole Constitution.

Whether a couple saved money, whether they kept the house clean—it was all Ford's concern. If they seemed to be having trouble, Ford was Mr. Fixit, trying to save their marriage, trying to make sure the man got home with his paycheck intact and not dissipated at a corner saloon or by a night out with some cutie.

To put a halo over this invasion of privacy, Ford hired a man who brought with him the sanctity of the church—Samuel S. Marquis, Dean of the Episcopal Cathedral of Detroit. The Reverend Mr. Marquis sent his teams of investigators into every home, and they were not appreciated, to say the least. And where the sociology department left off, the Big Brother at Ford's plants took over. That was called the service department.

It might as well have been called the "secret service department." It was headed by Harry Bennett, and it checked up on men on the assembly line, in the lunch rooms, and even in the rest rooms, to see if they were taking a short snort of booze or sneaking a cigarette.

Men actually were let go for smoking or drinking. About the time I was born the sociology department gave its last gasp, as Ford no longer was that interested in the private lives of his employees and concentrated more on his own private life, which certainly included my mother.

But if the sociology department was out of business, the service department grew by leaps and bounds under Bennett. It was said he had such an efficient spy system that practically every third man on the line was spying on the other two.

To show the kind of thing a man could be fired for, the folks talked about a particular employee who had dared to criticize something about Ford's car to his face; the man was trying to explain why car sales were going down.

Ford was furious and wanted the man fired, but knew it wouldn't look right to fire a man for an honest opinion. But the sociology department had learned that the man was having trouble with his wife, and so they fired him for that.

There was no union to appeal to. A company owner was king in those days.

I'm not saying all the men were saintly at Ford. There was a huge problem of thievery at the plants, and foxy Mr. Ford had to solve it some way. He came up with the unique solution of holding each foreman responsible for all the parts and machinery in his department. This cut down on pilferage tremendously, since nobody wanted to be fired for someone else's wrongdoing.

Ford hated to admit he was wrong about anything or even that he had made the slightest mistake. Once when some reporter caught him wearing shoes that were not mated, he quickly said, to Mother's amusement, that he frequently did that to remind himself of the days when he was poor.

When Ford did not want to see someone, he would do anything to get away. He was a master escape artist. Men around the plant would complain that they turned around and he was gone. He would be out a back door or side door. He was even known occasionally to make his escape through a window—on the ground floor, of course.

Sometimes he would say he needed to get something and would disappear. People waiting to see him would become furious and blame everyone else but Ford, sure that the other people were keeping them away from him, or vice versa. Of course in a way this was true. Ford had long lists of people he did not want to see, and woe be to the man—like Frank Campsall or Harry Bennett—who maneuvered it so Ford was forced to bump into the person he was avoiding.

Naturally, there were many people who were after huge donations for private or public charities, and Ford had a horror of being trapped, especially by a woman on the other side of the desk pleading for money for a good cause.

Ford's secretary would screen the people who were going to see Ford and extract from them a promise that they were not going to ask for money. It is amusing that when Rosika Schwimmer came to see Ford to tell him of her plan to stop World War I, she too had to promise she was not after money. What she was after ended up costing a whole lot more—a whole chartered ship and a month's pilgrimage.

Ford's refusal to give employees official titles was very puzzling. Men would look very sheepish if someone asked them what they did. Ford wanted them to be sort of a board of executives. Mother said if he gave them titles, someone might hire them away to another company.

It seemed to me that Ford got a little jealous of anyone who became too powerful—including Edsel—and not giving titles helped put people down. Edsel had the title of president, because that was something every company had to have. And if Henry didn't want to be president anymore, someone had to be.

I would notice that when men were asked at some of the Ford executive luncheons what they did, they would say something like, "Oh, I help look after the books," or "I take care of production problems," or "I help hire men." This kept them all sounding very humble, and I noticed Mr. Ford looked pleased.

If they dared ask Mr. Ford what *he* did, since his son was

now in charge, he would be most annoyed and would say with a faint, grim smile, "Oh, I let Edsel find something for me to do." Edsel would squirm. I am sure—and Mother frequently commented on it—that Edsel would have traded places with almost any other executive, rather than be a token president with an overachiever like Henry Ford looking over his shoulder.

It is really rather strange, and amusing, too, that even before I was born Henry Ford was using my name—John Dahlinger—when he was incognito. He would pose as Dad's uncle, and they would travel as Ray and John Dahlinger.

Any time Ford wanted to look at a piece of land or travel to some town because it had an historic house he wanted to buy, he was John Dahlinger.

When people ask me who I was named for, I have always said nobody, but I would always recall that I was named for Henry Ford's other self.

Some people thought Ford did not have a sense of humor. He certainly did, though it sometimes was a little unusual.

Ford had his own table in the executive dining room, and now and then he would have special luncheons. He would serve mountain oysters or rattlesnake meat. Not everyone was sophisticated enough to know what mountain oysters were, and some were quite shaken to find out after eating them that they were the testicles of young male calves, considered by some Western men to be a delicacy.

Sorensen, Ford's top production man, never curried favor with Ford by pretending to like the odd things he was serving. No matter what anyone else had, Sorensen always had steak.

I remember a particular time when I was about seven. I was playing with a toy car, and I ran it over Mr. Ford's shoe and up his leg. His hand stopped mine and he took the car. "You can't play with that car, John. It's not a Ford." He laughed and gave it back to me.

There were more rules around the plant than you could shake a stick at. C. H. Wills had his own solution to the ban on smoking—he simply chewed a cigar. Though it was never lighted, in a few hours the cigar was all in his mouth. He also had a spittoon.

To be close to Ford was to be aware of lots of cash. Ford had two safes in which he kept millions in cash. One safe was in his office in the engineering lab, and one was in the upstairs of the garage. Mother had the combination to the safe in the garage. Dad had the combination to both safes. I was told that there was $4 million in the garage safe and somewhat less in the office safe.

I never saw the office safe open, but I was with Dad and Henry Ford one time when they took several thousand dollars out of the garage safe. The safe was about four feet high; inside, it was almost solidly filled with cash, although I recall seeing some watches and a few other trinkets.

I don't think there were any bills smaller than a fifty; most of them were thousand- and hundred-dollar bills. It sounded as though they needed money to give to some man for information of some sort, but such things did not interest me at the time. I just thought it was rather neat to have so much ready cash.

In a way, Ford was a misogynist; he was always blaming some woman for what happened to a man. He had a theory that women were behind all evil, and I guess he didn't have to go further than the Bible to justify it.

When men were caught stealing things from the plant, or if he was interviewing an ex-convict for a job—Ford was famous for rehabilitating criminals—he would always ask if a woman wasn't at the bottom of it.

If the man said yes, he had only done it to please some woman or meet her demands, Ford would feel that the man was blameless and had learned his lesson and could have a job or could keep his job.

Along that line, I'll never forget Mother telling of an incident that amused her very much. A worker had stolen a new engine and other parts to renovate his old car. Everyone thought Ford would fire him instantly when it was drawn to his attention. But Ford, satisfied that the poor fellow had only been trying to please his unreasonable wife, who wanted a car that didn't stall on the road, found a new way to punish the man. He told him sternly to bring in his old motor and be quick about it.

In other words, the man got away scot-free, and only had to turn in the motor that he had thrown out anyway.

When unions started to enroll Ford workers, Mr. Ford became furious. "They can't do anything for my men that I'm not doing for them already," he said.

The workers disagreed. They thought a union would be able to stabilize their wages.

One of Ford's special pets helped keep the union away from Ford's doors a little longer by disrupting their meetings with tear gas. In the late '30s, Ford would be delighted to hear how John Gillespie had done it again—cleverly planting tear gas at the right moment so no union business could transpire.

Ford said it was an insult to a worker that he be expected to pay a union for the privilege of working in the Ford plant, or any factory. The man didn't need the union to get a job or to hold it, he claimed.

I well remember that my early teens were filled with talk of labor unions and Ford's troubles with them. Ford growled that the unions were out to get him and he was going to fight them all the way. He felt that he was already doing more for labor than anyone else had and that the unions were totally unreasonable to expect more. Hadn't Ford been the first man to pay a five-dollar day? It had been earthshaking when he had done it, and other companies had accused him of being a traitor for paying laborers so much money.

So Ford felt he had proven for all time that he was on the side of labor. He even came out and said he was not a capitalist, which made everybody around him laugh.

Furthermore, as Ford pointed out, hadn't he permitted men to work their way up to eight, nine, and ten dollars a day?

The trouble with this, the unions replied, was that Henry Ford would let everybody go when he closed down the plant to retool for a new model car, and then when he reopened everyone would be hired at the beginning wage and have to work his way up to eight, nine, and ten dollars again.

Henry Ford's reply to the union organizers was that he was no different from all the rest—all the auto manufacturers did the same thing. The issue was at an impasse. The unions wanted to organize the men at Ford plants and put them under contract, and Ford was not going to permit it.

By 1938, when I was fifteen, Ford was a holdout, since most other motor companies had given in and unionized. While pretending to stay aloof, Henry Ford was using various men in the company like Harry Bennett and John Gillespie—Bennett was head of security and Gillespie was a former water commissioner—to find out what the unions were up to.

Bennett used the friendly approach, getting cozy with the president of United Auto Workers, Homer Martin; John Gillespie used the opposite approach, being belligerent and getting himself arrested for harassing union officials and breaking up meetings.

Eventually, the situation became complicated beyond belief. Ford was paying out cash to union finks and spies outside the union. And because of the National Labor Relations Board, Ford was enmeshed in court cases involving all the assembly plants.

The union troubles dragged along. Ford told the men around him that he was sure there was a Jewish plot to get him and that the unions were the device being used. He thought the unions were being run by Jews, and it was hard for anyone to convince him otherwise, even though he knew that the top unionists—Phil Murray, John L. Lewis, and Bill Green—were not Jewish.

Ford was in favor of using tear gas to keep union organizers and demonstrators from setting foot on Ford property. Edsel was horrified at the very thought of such violence and for once countermanded Ford's order.

The strike led by the CIO took place in 1941, and the plant was closed for at least a month. Only Ford and a few high executives dared go into the Rouge. Edsel was not among them.

I am sure Ford wished his son had been made of tougher stuff. But by this time Edsel was in very poor health.

Ford was spending a fortune on lawyers, both his own team, headed by Colombo, and outside lawyers from New York. Typically, Ford, all of a sudden and with no particular warning, switched and decided to let the unions in. "If you can't lick them, join them," he said, and that is what he did.

In June 1941, with World War II already blazing in Europe, Ford signed a contract with the UAW. The amusing thing is that once Ford gave in, he went all the way, giving the unions much more than they had asked for. As a matter of fact, he went so far in the other direction that again other auto executives thought he had lost his mind. As he said at our house, he just wanted to get rid of the problem once and for all so the unions would not keep coming back asking for more. He thrilled the unions by deciding that Ford would do the paperwork and check off the union dues from each worker. Ford's reason, as he explained to us, was that it was better for the worker to be tied to Ford in a package deal, with Ford playing banker with the union.

When I read of new negotiations of union contracts every few years and of new union troubles between the unions and Ford Motor Company, I always think of how wrong Ford was to think that one contract could be it for all time.

And I remember how proud Ford was that in his contract he volunteered to pay his men more than other auto companies paid their men. It must be said, however, that Ford guessed wrong about how unions would grow. He thought the union movement would destroy itself through internecine wars.

"They'll never be able to get along with each other," he said.

11
Henry Ford Builds His Dream Houses

Some people collect butterflies. Some, matchbook covers. Henry Ford collected homes.

As if to make up for his lack of roots as a child or the fact that he could not trace his ancestry on his mother's side, he insisted on owning all the homes that had meaning for him—and a few that hadn't.

He moved the house in which he was born to Greenfield Village. By good fortune Fairlane was near the square house he had lived in when he first married. It had been built on land his father gave him.

That square house was carefully refurnished to look exactly the way it had when Ford had built it, using lumber from his own sawmill.

Dad took over Mother's job while she occupied herself helping Ford to make his great dream come true: to build a whole village as a museum of his past. Ford knew that his fame would extend far into the future and would increase with years. "History is a lot of bunk," he would tell me. "You're not appreciated until you're dead, and then they get it all wrong on why you should be appreciated."

One reason that Ford wanted to reconstruct Greenfield Village was to pay tribute to his mother. He had never got over her death and would talk about her quite a bit.

It's amusing that the man who was responsible for the paving of roads all over the nation and the world made sure that in one corner of the world near him the roads would remain dirt, to remind him of his childhood. In fact, as the nation was building paved roads and superhighways, that man was happily adding to his network of dirt roads as he collected houses and other structures and hauled them to his dream village.

When Ford moved Edison's shop to Greenfield Village, he was so meticulous that he even brought some of the ground and debris that had been outside the original Menlo Park lab.

He reconstructed, exactly, the slave cabin in which George Washington Carver had lived. His excuse for this particular structure was that Carver was coming to visit and he didn't want him to be embarrassed because it was hard for a Negro to find lodgings.

When he came, Ford insisted that Carver use the front door and not the back door of Ford's home, as Carver was inclined to do—he would not go so far as to invite him to stay overnight in his home, yet he would build him his own cabin. Ford told him when he started to walk around to the back of Fairlane, "No friend of mine goes in the back door."

Though Carver, Ford liked to say, was much impressed and very happy to sleep in a slave-quarter replica, I always felt he might have been a little insulted.

Mr. Ford was much impressed with Carver and brought him to school. I remember looking at Carver as he talked to us. We did not see many black people, so he was a novelty to our school assembly. I remember he told us how wonderful the peanut was—one of the greatest creations of God. It could feed us and shelter us; there was practically nothing you could not do with the peanut or its hull.

Afterwards, I remember Ford's telling me that the peanut was a very fine plant, but the greatest gift from God was wheat, the staff of life.

So there was the Carver house in the Ford collection of homes; and there was Fairlane, where, we used to say, Ford was "in residence at the castle"—but not in his hearing.

Nor did Mr. Ford hear what we said about his most outrageous house project—Ways, Georgia.

To understand Ways, you first have to know that it was utter swampland when it came to Ford's attention. The reason Ford built it in the first place is that he lost interest in Fort Myers after Edison died. I have a postcard sent to Mother and Dad from the Fords when they were at their winter home next door to the Edisons. It shows that the Florida estate was well secluded, with two rows of trees along a drive.

So after looking the country over for a number of years, in spite of all the beautiful and feasible land they could have had with their unlimited wealth, they chose the swamps of Georgia. Actually, what folks said about Ways is that if God were going to give the world an enema, that is where he would insert the tube.

Of course, this only made the Ways swampland a greater challenge to Ford. He had a dream, and he was going to prove that he could make dry land out of a swamp. The world, he was sure, was going to thank him for it in time.

For months men pumped out the water. Then came the snakes. And the bugs. He sprayed bugs and he shot snakes and he built a beautiful house in the middle of the carnage. And he planted beautiful grass.

But he could never get rid of the snakes, and he couldn't get rid of the bugs either. The house was only livable a few months of the winter. He and Mrs. Ford would arrive there with high hopes, but they would have to leave in March because the bugs were so bad they couldn't stand it.

Mother would say it was the darndest thing to watch those snakes. As the men mowed the lawn, snakes went flying into the air like confetti. It was raining snakes.

In Dad's office—I don't know what happened to it after the purge—was a huge rattlesnake skin, at least five feet long, mounted on a plaque. Mother had killed it. She was a crack shot.

Clara Ford was absolutely thrilled with her Ways house. She should have been; one of the most amusing letters I have from Mother's collection is the carbon copy of the letter Mother wrote to explain to the architect all the changes Mrs. Ford wanted made in her house plans.

The poor man must have torn his hair out. The year was 1936, and the Fords were in the middle of building Mrs. Ford's dream house in the swamps of Georgia. This house was going to be her house, with everything *she* wanted, just as Fairlane was Ford's dream house and was supposed to have reflected everything he wanted.

Mother was a go-between, finding out what Mrs. Ford wanted and then explaining it to the letter to the beleaguered architect and builder.

Henry Ford Farms
Dearborn, Mich.

May 29, 1936

Ray Dahlinger, Mgr.
Telephone Walnut 5

Mr. Cletus W. Bergen,
Savannah, Georgia.

Dear Mr. Bergen:

It may seem a long time before getting word back to you, but we have only been home two weeks and one has to wait till the right people get into the right place at the right time, but let's get going. Mrs. Ford is still all enthused about the residence and just knows it will be through in time.

Starting with the first floor, you will notice the partitions between Mr. and Mrs. Ford's dressing rooms have been moved approximately a foot in order to give Mrs. F a bit more space in her room. In the service dining room, the china cabinet has been extended the depth of the icebox whatever it finally is, in this way it makes more of a separation between kitchen and dining room. The icebox will perhaps be built up, in any event it will take up all the space between present sink and icebox.

On the second floor we had lots of fun and hope the changes don't in any way interfere with construction—Starting with the Master Bedroom—Mrs. Ford was a bit worried about wall space for dressers, so we moved the doors into both her and Mr. Ford's clothes closets in order to get the desired space giving approximately six feet of wall on either side of the door.

Now in Mr. F's bathroom we took closet that was in servant's room and made it open into bathroom, Mrs. Ford was quite pleased with this because it made more room for shirts, underwear, hose, etc., she said, from this I take it this closet would be in the nature of a built-in chest of drawers perhaps, I will measure some here at the residence that are used for that purpose and send to you, it might be of some help. Of course in doing all this it necessitated the moving of the wash basin which I presume will meet with your approval.

Now then, in Mrs. Ford's bath she would like the water-closet and wash basin reversed and a much bigger basin as I told you when down there I expected she would, but more of that later.

Now in the bedroom across the hall from the servants' room, Mrs. F said she hadn't put a whole lot of thought on that one so after looking it over found by putting tub at other end of bathroom so door could go closer in corner of room we could gain a lot more wall space, if the wash basin or toilet is next to tub I don't believe matters, whichever is most convenient for you.

Now the other bedroom—#3 on the drawings—Mrs. F wants to sort of play with it, by that I mean, fix it up real old-fashioned, big four-poster bed, chintz, old dresser, etc. etc., now she thought it would look nicer if the outside wall was uniform, that is windows and walls (don't get worried this doesn't interfere with the outside) that is why we moved the partition into the bathroom.

Will this interfere in any way with truss or brace for ceiling below, hope not. Mrs. F realizes it makes a jog in the wall where the closet is but doesn't mind that so much as the windows not being spaced evenly.

Now that is the explanation of the markings on the drawings. Expect to be down there very soon to settle the kitchen and the bunk house and am looking forward with interest to talking this all over with you. When you make revised drawings will you please send Mrs. Ford a plain set just like these I am returning to you, she was very pleased with them.

She is a bit troubled about the slop sink being in the downstairs hall but hasn't had time to think of a new place. The china cabinets in the dining room should be four feet across the front, the reason for this is that she likes one that is in a friend's house and I went over and measured it and it was four feet.

I am enclosing my very, very rough sketch, will explain it when I come down. Mrs. F didn't say it had to be a duplicate of the cupboard except for width, but if she does, will have a better sketch made.

Now about the hotel plans, they look so much better don't they? Mr. Voorheis thought so too, but suggested that the post be taken out of the kitchen, that could be done, couldn't we use an iron beam to support the roof, that isn't a very long span?

You will notice we have reversed the linen closet and storage room off the kitchen entry. Will go into all details as to the why of all these changes when I go down. May take out storage room in other end of kitchen and make it all kitchen, perhaps switching sink around and putting a door into pantry there also.

The two bedrooms on both floors at the side toward Mrs. Gills (I don't know North or South down there) would have more room for twin beds if there was only one window in the end, there are plenty of windows anyway. Now at the other end of the hall and across from the living room of the suite, we changed the door to make more room for beds. That hall works out so nicely there doesn't it?

The women's washroom on the first floor seems very narrow, couldn't we widen it out a bit and make the dressing room narrower, think it's almost necessary for anyone standing at the wash basins. Now in the men's room perhaps the floor could be moved front a bit to give more room in front of wash stands, or stands could be put on Lounge wall.

Now upstairs—starting from Mrs. Gills' direction—the linen

closet doors could be brought out, with shelves along each side. The bedrooms to either side, the windows in center of wall as I said earlier in letter. The bedroom—the marks you see to move the bath door I'll go into with you later.

Now the bedroom next to the women's room, seems like one big window would give more air than two small ones, and we changed the door to put beds on other wall. In the women's room, two feet seems very narrow between basins and doors, perhaps we could steal six inches on either partition, what do you think? I dislike seeing doors to men's rooms and ladies' rooms right next to each other, of course we could switch entrance to men's room and that would bring it right next to dance hall floor, don't know which would be the most objectionable, but think about this will you. In the bedroom across hall we changed door to give more room.

You know if I don't stop pretty soon this will rival your fifteen page letter, but don't worry I'm stopping now. But this will give you a chance to think things over and will talk it out just as soon as we go down which I expect will be in a very few days. Will save what Mrs. F had to say about bathrooms till I get down but it's good news. So best regards, and I'll be seeing you.

Yours very truly,
Evangeline Dahlinger
(signed)

Henry Ford was annoyed that he couldn't trace his maternal ancestry, because his mother had been adopted. That was a rather tragic story. Both her parents had died within a short time of each other, her father in an accident and her mother, I believe, through illness.

Ford spent thousands of dollars trying to unravel the mystery, but, to my knowledge, never found out who her ancestors had been.

So much did Ford care about his past that he even had transported to Greenfield Village the old log cabin in which, according to the story around Dearborn, a hermit had lived near his childhood home. Ford had gone to visit the hermit when he was a little boy and had had long conversations with him. Early in life, Ford gained a reverence for nature from the old man.

When I was a year old Mother left me for the first time to go to Sudbury, Massachusetts, to the Wayside. Inn, which Henry Ford was renovating. When I was eighteen months old, Nanny took me to another place that he was renovating, the Botsford Inn, an old coaching stop near Farmington, Michigan.

Those projects were unusual for that period in Ford's life because he didn't take the buildings with him. But he did bring back something just as interesting—a dance master.

At Sudbury Inn Ford was carried away by old-fashioned dances like the quadrille and square dancing. He brought Benjamin Lovett back to Greenfield Village and installed him in a corner of the engineering lab. Lovett taught Mr. and Mrs. Ford, and every friend who could be corralled, all the old steps.

I got my share of bowing and mincing when Ford decided the old dances should be mandatory at school. Eventually, he built Lovett Hall at the Village, where 200 to 300 people could dance at a time—Ford among them.

This is the only time Ford named a hall for any of his teachers—it would be a dancing teacher.

As for Botsford Inn, Ford was preserving it because it was one of the oldest surviving stagecoach stops in Michigan. Later he moved the Clinton Inn, another stagecoach stop, to Greenfield Village.

Ford's renovations depended on what he had read that day in the newspapers or what someone had told him. At age one, I was not too interested in what he was doing at Sudbury, but later on I learned he had redone that inn because he'd heard it had an old water wheel and he was fascinated by water power, as proven by all the water generators throughout the state.

Later he contributed large amounts of money to the Berry School in Rome, Georgia, because Mrs. Edison told him that someone should do something for the underprivileged, and how sad it was to be a little Southern child attending this particular school.

While Ford was traveling with, I believe, Edison and some of their cronies, he heard that "Mary Had a Little Lamb" had been written at a place called Redstone Hill. He got all excited, especially since that little nursery rhyme was in his favorite schoolbook, *McGuffey's Second Reader*.

The story of how that nursery rhyme came about intrigued the folk historian in him. It seemed that a girl named Mary Elizabeth Sawyer had attended a little wooden school that had benches and crude writing desks. Not only was the building painted red, but it stood on Redstone Hill. The incident involving Mary took place sometime between 1790 and 1856, when the school was abandoned.

According to the story Ford learned, one morning the minister's nephew was visiting the school, which was a big deal. Unfortunately, on that particular day Mary's pet lamb had chosen to follow her to school and into the classroom, and it had disrupted the class.

Though the teacher was annoyed by Mary's little lamb, which "made the children laugh and play, which was against the rule," the nephew was delighted and wrote the poem which made his name famous in its time: John Roulstone.

Sometimes Ford would acquire—and bring home in triumph and at great expense—a house that would later turn out to be a mistake. The Stephen Foster house was probably such an experience. Few tourists who visit it have any reason to doubt its authenticity. However, after he had spared no expense to transport the lovely shuttered white house, Mother received a copy (which I still have) of the letter written by an irate member of the Foster family claiming that it was the wrong house.

So irate was the relative, a granddaughter or grandniece, that she sent copies of the letter to about half a dozen officials connected with the Village.

But nothing deterred Ford from the thrill of house collecting. Come to think of it, this showed again how history gets botched and twisted and glossed over, so that people don't know whether a simple thing like a famous house is the true one. This time Ford helped history become bunk.

Here is the letter challenging the authenticity of the Stephen Foster house:

8323 Epworth Blvd.
Detroit, Michigan
May 26, 1936

Mr. William J. Cameron
Engineering Department
Ford Motor Company
Dearborn, Michigan

My Dear Sir:

I have recently read a two-installment article in the Edison Institute paper, the Herald, entitled "A Biography of Stephen C. Foster," written by a young student of the Institute, Miss Isabelle C. Gassett.

It is a good thing that Miss Gassett had a copy of my father Morrison Foster's "Biography of Stephen C. Foster" on which to base her essay—at least, in this way many truths about Stephen C. Foster were introduced into the mass of history faking which recently has been handed out to the Greenfield Village school children in order to bolster up Mr. Henry Ford's bogus Stephen Foster birthplace.

This article in the Herald indicates that instead of acknowledging the fact that Mr. Ford's house is spurious, the officers of Greenfield Village have determined to save Mr. Ford's face in this stupid affair even if they have to enlist the aid of every innocent little school child in Greenfield Village.

Pretty small business for a big man like Mr. Ford, Mr. Cameron. How much nobler it would have been to tell the children the Truth about this house right from the start.

Yours very truly,
Mrs. Evelyn F. Morneweck
(signed)

cc Miss Isabelle C. Gassett
Miss Barbara Sheldrick
Mrs. Ray Dahlinger √
Mr. Wm. A. Simonds
Mr. Frank Campsall
Dr. Lee McCollester

I was six or seven when Henry Ford designated me to lay the first brick of the wall surrounding Greenfield Village. That was 1930, but the Village didn't open officially until 1933, when I was ten.

Ford made sure to honor his friends. As soon as you enter the museum building, you see a specially framed large square of cement in the floor, with a shovel sticking up from it. That is the shovel used by Luther Burbank, who would lead Ford and his buddies Edison and Firestone on nature hikes.

Also in the square are Thomas Edison's footprints; Edison himself knelt down and wrote his name large in the wet cement: "Thos A Edison Sept 27 1928."

Rumor had it that Ford wanted to have a sample of the kind of house that the original Pilgrims had left behind when they came to the New World. So he went to England and found the perfect Cotswold stone cottage, which dated back to the early seventeenth century.

It was just a little cottage, but the work that went into moving it stone by stone was tremendous. Ford brought over a craftsman named Gus Murchow, who understood this kind of structure. Money was no object and he made sure it had everything a Cotswold cottage should have: monk's chair, Bible chest, wooden plates, leather jugs for water, canopy bed, pigeons to nest in the eaves, and Lancashire sheep to graze around it.

Somewhere along the line Ford decided he should have something of Lincoln's. By a wonderful coincidence he heard that the old Logan County courthouse in which Lincoln had practiced law was still around. He grabbed it and had it hauled to Greenfield, and when Herbert Hoover came to the ceremony opening Menlo Park laboratory, he lighted the fire in the fireplace, which was intended to become an eternal flame.

It is hard to imagine how many houses Ford fell in love with and collected. There must be an inventory of them somewhere, though I don't have it. Going to school at the Village, as I did, I had to live and go to school in some of his collections, and I played in and around others.

He had collected just about everything left to collect, it seemed. But then the ultimate collector of houses collected the ultimate house—old dog Tray's doghouse.

The insatiable Ford located the little house that had belonged to that faithful dog—"grief cannot drive him away"—and planted it as tenderly on the grounds of Greenfield Village as he did the grandest house of his collection. It even had a canine in residence. Its name? Tray, of course.

12
"Quadrupeds Are Out"

Ford cars and silk shirts were the status symbols of the Roaring Twenties. Tom Beck, the president of Crowell-Collier Publishing Company, was well aware of symbols. He was, in fact, obsessed with what he had missed by not following Ford. He had turned down a chance to invest in Ford in those early days, saying Ford's cars were "impractical."

Later, of course, he agonized over the path not taken. As a result, when aviation arrived, he invested early, commenting that he wasn't going to miss out twice.

Beck and Ford were friends, and to him, as well as to me, Ford confided that the world of the future would be a world without animals. "Quadrupeds are out," he said.

Ford summed it up in his later years: "We don't need horses. We've got the tractor. We've got the automobile. We don't need cows—we can make synthetic milk. We can make meat substitute out of soybean and coconuts—you can hardly tell the difference. We don't need sheep. We will be able to make wool out of synthetic things—it'll be better than wool."

I know it sounds a little crazy, but I really think half of Ford's inventions were aimed at thwarting animals and cheating them out of an honest living. If he could have walked up to every cow and horse in the world and said, "You're fired," he'd have considered it a day well spent.

He was a lot like W. C. Fields about pets; he didn't like them. He did have a few dogs at Fairlane, but they were kept at the stables. He had a Newfoundland at the Cotswold cottage for atmosphere. He had a pair of Dalmatians to run along with the horse-drawn coaches—anything for authenticity.

There were always things happening with the dogs; one would die or get killed or run away. Replacements for the Village dogs were kept at our house. I recall we always had a spare pair of Dalmatians, and once I took care of their litter of puppies.

Ford had good reason to distrust horses. He told me that when he was a young boy, his foot caught in the stirrup when a horse bolted. He was dragged around and could have been killed. I don't recall ever seeing him ride a horse, and when we would watch Mother riding, he would tell me how stupid and dangerous a horse was, and how I must never approach a horse from behind, but always from the front so the horse could see me—something I already knew but politely listened to.

Ford considered the horse a very inefficient instrument. He called it a thousand-pound hay-burning motor with one-horse power.

I still have a card with a typed comment about the horse. It was either typed up by Mother as a defense of the horse to show the Boss, or else it was something Henry Ford brought to our house to show how dumb horses are. I haven't a clue as to who is being quoted.

A FACT

"INTELLIGENCE" of a horse is simply a reflection of the intelligence of the man who has taught him the habits he possesses.

"A horse cannot put two and two together," Mr. Ford would say. "The world would be better off without horses. They can see you every day of their lives and still kick you to death. A tractor is a little better, but even with a tractor you have to be careful."

Tractors could be dangerous, because if the plow hit a stone or a stump, it could jackknife back and throw a man off, possibly crushing him. When the Ferguson improvement, a device that held the plow and tractor rigidly together as one unit, came on the market, Ford was very interested.

I really think one reason Ford worked so hard on his car inventions and on the Fordson tractor was that he had it in for the horse ever since that horse threw him. Even so, since I was crazy about riding, he gave me many horses through the years. But he would sit and tell me, when I was a little boy, how terrible and mean horses were and would warn me never to put my trust in a horse.

I solemnly assured him that I never would, but just once I did, and the same thing happened to me as had happened to him —I fell off the horse, with my foot still in the stirrup, and the horse would not stop. Luckily my boot came off, so I was not dragged a half-mile, as he had been as a child.

Anyway, it was a little hard to understand why I should hate horses when both Mother and Dad rode horseback and drove sulkies. Mother loved to dress in riding clothes. When she flew, all she added to her riding habit were goggles, helmet, and silk scarf.

Mother liked to be either on a horse or in a plane, and many is the time Ford would have to wait around for Mother to come back from riding or flying.

Sometimes when Mother would go racing off on her horse, as I grew older I felt that she was probably meeting Mr. Ford somewhere.

As Henry Ford worked toward his great vision of a world that had no need of quadrupeds, I was his guinea pig. And I wasn't the only one. Everyone had to eat the strange concoctions he was putting together and calling milk, meat, and vegetables, depending on their color. Soybean milk was his triumph. I had to drink it while he asked me eagerly, "Can you tell the difference? Isn't that a fine glass of milk?"

I loved milk, but his soybean milk almost cured me. It tasted like chalk. I was perfectly satisfied with the job a cow did, and his version was simply terrible. For a time, Ford was eating so much of the ersatz foods he was concocting that Mrs. Ford worried about his health.

Ford would eat soybean pie and drink the soybean milk that made even milk of magnesia taste good. Ford was working on a soybean body for an automobile. They used to say that if it didn't run, Ford could eat it.

Mother joined in the laughter, but Ford was undeterred. He was trying to make a plastic substitute for steel. At the time, the plastic substitute was so much more costly than steel that it didn't make sense. But history has proven him right.

I remember when Ford had the back trunk of his car made of soybean plastic, and he would hammer it with an ax to show how strong it was.

Unfortunately, once in the middle of one of his demonstration tryouts the thing cracked.

Ford's ultimate triumph along the soybean line was the soybean dinner he himself dreamed up and had served at the time of the Ford exhibit at the *Chicago Century of Progress Fair* in August 1934.

As you will see, every single item on the menu was made of soybean, in part or in toto:

Soybean–tomato juice cocktail

Celery stuffed with Soybean cheese   Salted Soybeans

Puree of Soybean   Soybean crackers

Soybean croquettes with tomato sauce

Buttered green Soybeans

Pineapple ring with Soybean cheese

and Soybean dressing

Soybean bread with Soybean butter
Apple pie (Soybean crust)
Cocoa with Soybean milk   Soybean coffee
Assorted Soybean cookies   Soybean cakes
Assorted Soybean candy

I was about eleven when Ford was at the peak of his excitement about soybeans. You had only to talk to him for five minutes and soybeans would enter the conversation. He kept bottles of soybean milk in our refrigerator in case he got thirsty and in case I weakened enough to drink a little too. I only drank it, however, under the greatest duress.

I still have the recipe he gave to Mother for making soybean milk. The formula was developed by his chemical engineers, but it was his taste buds that determined when they had the right formula:

Soak one-half pound soybeans overnight and grind to a fine powder. Add two quarts of water and heat in a double boiler for one-half hour. Strain liquid through a fine cloth and season with a dash of salt. Add one or two tablespoons of syrup to sweeten. A dash of banana oil can also be added to make it resemble cow's milk a little more closely.

Ford was always shifting the formula around a trifle to see which sweetening syrup was best—maple or sorghum or honey—and whether a little more or less salt would improve the taste.

Ford was evangelical about soybeans. He talked of how cooked soybeans tasted much better than lima beans did, and how soybean spread was much better for children than peanut butter. He advised me to try it in a soybean and jelly sandwich.

Ford urged Mother to tell our cook to use a lot of soybeans in cooking and to overcome the strong flavor of the beans by adding plenty of onions. In his own household the cooks were ordered to sneak a few soybeans into every food on the table—into soup, salad, the peas or other vegetable of the day.

Ford would now and then flash a letter around from some doctor or other who was grateful for Ford's experiments with soybean milk because babies who were allergic to cow's milk were able to use inexpensive, life-saving soybean milk. And also those adults who were allergic to milk were able to enjoy puddings and things that they had never been able to enjoy before.

Incidentally, Ford's son was named after the man who was in charge of food research at Ford, Doctor Edsel Ruddiman. Ruddiman worked in the engineering lab and was one of Ford's favorite people.

Their friendship went back many years to when Henry Ford was a child at school and shared his seat with Edsel Ruddiman.

Ford, of course, worked closely with Dr. Ruddiman in maximizing the uses of soybeans. First they extracted the oil, which was used in salads or for cooking. Then they made flour with the dried beans. I got so confused with all the soybean flour being hauled into the house and school that I never knew whether I was eating wheat bread and cookies or whether something very delicious looking, like a frosted cake or muffin, was partly or totally soybean. I was happier not knowing.

Nowadays soybeans are very respectable, and nobody laughs when they see toasted, salted soybeans right next to the salted peanuts in a store. When I see them there I never fail to think of Ford and how pleased he would be.

I don't believe we see soybean cottage cheese, which he also fancied, but soybeans are becoming an important part of many manufactured foods and are being widely used as a meat "extender." But in his day Ford had to take a lot of abuse and be the butt of many jokes and newspaper cartoons for his belief in the soybean.

It is too bad Mr. Ford could not have lived to see the vindication of his vision of a soybean economy in which soybeans would feed and serve man in many ways. For example, I recall that Ford told me that some day plastics made of soybeans would be used instead of wood to make beautiful furniture.

He also thought that since people liked shiny cars, they could make automobile bodies of plastic and not have to waste time, energy, and money polishing them. Ford men came up with molds in which curved objects could be made from soybean plastic, and he spent several million dollars for a building at the Rouge in which plastics were manufactured for such things as gearshift knobs and auto horns.

If I recall correctly, Ford at one time had twenty thousand acres of soybeans under cultivation under Dad's direction, and it was said he was spending over a million dollars a year experimenting with the plant in various ways—as food, as plastic, as animal food, as a high-protein, low-calorie diet food, and as a source of industrial oils. Ford would brag about how there was nothing in the soybean plant that was wasted; even the stalk could be made into fiber.

As Ford saw the world of the future—and I'm sorry it didn't come to pass—every farmer would become wealthy by running his own little factory, or "cottage industry," as Ford called it. He would produce soybeans in his field and make at least one soybean product for sale to factories or grocery stores.

As Ford foresaw the world, farmers wouldn't need barns. "With no animals, there need be no buildings on a farm except the granaries," he said. Except, of course, the little farm factories. Actually, Ford did help some farmers set up such small industries, but they died out when he grew too old to take a personal interest. As I recall, one of Ford's triumphs was to develop enamel paint that utilized the soybean.

I was always surprised at the unlikely substances Ford got from vegetables. For example, he extracted oil from watermelon and cantaloupe seeds.

Ford came up with a felt-type lining for auto interiors which was made from cornstalks and various straws that were useless field waste. It could be pressed into any form, so that it fit the interior like a glove, and it was more attractive than felt cloth.

It is amusing to look back and realize that Henry Ford may have been breaking the law, because he was growing marijuana for experimental reasons. He was growing all kinds of things to see what properties they had that could help him shape the world of the future. He was going to get rubber out of milkweed, for example, and we had a lot of that.

The marijuana was enclosed by a large cyclone fence. The Ford people thought it had all been destroyed after Ford died, but some years ago they found it growing wild again.

Henry Ford truly believed that in the world of the future only a small portion of time would be spent in earning the money needed to live—only about two percent of a person's time.

"Earning a living," he said, "will be the smallest part of our troubles." He believed that most of what man needed would be manufactured from crops grown in the fields—especially soybeans. "The farm and the factory are common allies," he said.

For a time Ford held the carrot in almost as high regard as he later held the soybean. I was told that when I was three or four, he ate a whole dinner from soup to dessert in which every dish on the menu was made of carrots. About the time I was going off to Deerfield Academy, Ford was getting very excited about wheat again as the ultimate food that would make a human live a tremendously long life.

Ford would comment that he planned to live at least a hundred years and that anyone and everyone could do the same by keeping poisons out of their systems. And when he said poisons, he meant fresh breadstuffs as well as alcohol and cigarette smoke.

His campaign against the quadruped never quite ceased. He was forever sounding off against four-footed animals, especially those that provided meat. As early as 1919 or '20 he had said the world would be better off without meat, because "it's 75 percent ashes anyway." And he further insulted the cow by calling it "the crudest machine in the world."

Toward the end of his life, having become disenchanted with churches that were always after money and having developed his various religious prejudices, he amended his statement a little. He had to be dissuaded from issuing a statement to the press that said, "Cows, pigs, horses, and creeds will someday disappear from the face of the earth."

13
My Career, Apart from Henry Ford

I didn't run away from home at the age of fifteen, the way Henry Ford had, but I wasn't far behind. At sixteen I made my break to freedom and the outer world, escaping Mr. Ford's all-pervasive presence by going all the way to Deerfield, Massachusetts, when I was in the tenth grade.

I would have gone in the ninth grade, but first I had to convince Mother how important this was to me. Mother thought that anything she wanted could easily be handled through her Ford connections, but she had never been up against the likes of Deerfield's famous headmaster, Frank L. Boyden, who was like a rock and didn't care about anybody's connections. Everybody at Deerfield Academy had great connections.

Anyway, by the time she got started on her campaign to get me in, it was too late to wear him down, and I had to continue at Greenfield Village, going to the first year of high school at Edison Institute.

My Career, Apart from Henry Ford

I went away to school in 1939, the same year Henry Ford had his first stroke. He was seventy-six. He was not happy when I went away. He had wanted me to continue at Edison, but I was hell-bent to get into Deerfield Academy. Once I got there, I hated it. I had come in my second year of high school and was far behind the others. Ford had put the emphasis on practical education, and we had only gone to school four and a half days a week. The other half-day we had spent doing useful technical work.

But I stuck it out, somehow. It was always assumed that I'd work for Ford. It was not until Ford was dead that I got a realistic look at the world as it was to those who didn't have a friendly old billionaire hovering over them. I went to Mrs. Ford, who spoke to Henry II. He arranged for me to be a manufacturer's representative with a company that did business with Ford. But that's getting ahead of the story. I want to take it from the top.

I have come across Mother's correspondence with Mr. Boyden from the summer of 1938, and now that it no longer matters that I failed to get in that year, it's interesting to look back and see how Mother operated; perhaps the reader would like this insight into the mind that intrigued Henry Ford.

Mother seems to have started with a telegram informing the headmaster that her son had chosen his school. She was a little rocked back on her heels to get the following reply from headmaster Boyden, and I know that I was crushed:

My dear Mrs. Dahlinger:

Thank you for your telegram of August 19th. I am sorry but we do not publish a catalogue, as we always arrange for a personal interview before accepting any boys.

At the present time our enrollment is complete and we do not now anticipate any changes before the opening of school. I should, however, be very glad to help you about some other good school in New England, if you wish; in which case, I should know more about your son's character, personality, and scholastic standing.

The last I knew there was still room for boys at the Berkshire School, the Choate School, Governor Dummer Academy, Lawrenceville, and Taft. All of these are excellent schools and are arranged alphabetically, not in any order of preference. Choate, Lawrenceville, and Taft are larger institutions with an enrollment of from three to five hundred. Berkshire and Governor Dummer Academy have about one hundred and twenty-five boys.

I hope you will not hesitate to let me help you in any possible way.

Cordially yours,
(signed)

Mother quickly phoned headmaster Boyden to urge him to see if there wasn't room for just one more student. She used her tried and true technique of concern and good fellowship.

He held out scant hope. Even so, Mother tried a second technique, firing off a three-page letter to him before his reply could reach her:

Dear Mr. Boyden:

Not having heard from you regarding John's entrance at Deerfield, we are hoping that "no news is good news." Also I thought that it might be better if I made an effort to more fully explain our telephone conversation.

You may have wondered why we didn't start in May making arrangements about schools, as most people do? Last May John didn't particularly care about his education, it was only two years or so back that he would say, "I'm not going to waste my time going to college, the heck with it."

Going on the idea that colleges are overcrowded with many that would rather be doing something else, that are better fitted to work with their hands, shall we say, I kept very silent when John would make the above statement. However, little by little, he has given it more thought and this summer when he again brought up the subject of going away to school, I suggested stopping at a few schools while on our trip.

Edsel Ford.

Here I am in Palm Beach
after the war.

Henry Ford strikes a pose familiar to all who knew him.

"Make hay while the sun shines"—something Mr. Ford most certainly did.

"Keep the home fires burning." Mr. Ford poses before the fire in one of the Greenfield Village buildings.

The original *Spirit of St. Louis,* flown by Lindbergh to Dearborn in 1927 after his historic flight. Next to the plane is the Ford Flivver, Harry Brooks's favorite "toy," which had been built by Brooks, Shorty Schroder and Dad. Lindbergh flew the Flivver during that visit; to my knowledge only Brooksie, Lindbergh and I have ever flown the Flivver.

Igor Sikorsky and Mr. Ford look over Sikorsky's VS-300, his first successful helicopter. Mr. Sikorsky flew the helicopter onto the green at Greenfield Village and then presented it to Mr. Ford for the Henry Ford Museum. Ford admired Sikorsky for pioneering rotary wing flight.

Mother and Mr. Ford.

Mother on a fun cart, at the reins of one of our harness horses. When she was on the sulky she could beat just about everyone—even the trainer. Once, when Mother was the loser, she whispered in my ear, "I have to let the men win once in a while."

Mother at the christening of the USS *Dearborn* on September 24, 1933.

Mr. Ford and Dad surveying construction of the Willow
Run plant, June 30, 1941.

Two midget racing cars Dad built in our workshop.

Dad enjoyed a long-lasting personal friendship with
Henry Ford, from 1907 until Ford's death in 1947. In this
picture Dad is flanked by Mr. Ford and Henry II. From
the moment the younger Henry took over the company, Dad
was caught up in the power struggle. His usefulness to the
company and the family terminated with Mrs. Ford's death
in 1950. The key was turned in the lock so quickly that he
was unable to recover many of his personal possessions
from the storeroom behind his office.

Mr. and Mrs. Henry Ford.

Will you understand that he made up his mind that it would be best for him, that it wasn't his parents that said "Now, John, we're going to send you to school because, etc., etc."

And because it was his own decision, that is why I think he will honestly try and will get all he can out of it, more than some boy that was just sent. Wish you could have heard his reasoning, I just listened and didn't say a word.

"It will teach me to study, to concentrate, to like to read." "I'll really get my lessons there. There won't be the distractions that there are here, won't be some place that you'd rather go at night than study." "I'll meet new people, be in a different section of the country, later I'd like to go to a Western School perhaps, and then when I was older no matter from what part of the country a person came I might meet, I could better understand them." This may all sound very rambly to you, but it's the mind of a fifteen year old expressing himself out loud.

Mr. Dahlinger and I have worked for the Ford Motor Company and Mr. Henry Ford since we were both quite young, Mr. Dahlinger in the Transportation Department and I as a secretary. Since our marriage we have managed the Farms and helped build up the Village, therefore John is "the boss's kid." It would do him good to get away from this, not because it has spoiled him but because of the fact we have always said "well, you better not do this or that or have this or that because if you do it or have it others will think they can too." This hasn't harmed him in any way perhaps, it may have been a help in being thoughtful of others and not taking advantage, but there does come a time when enough is enough.

I didn't go into all this with Mr. Allen because yours was the first school at which we stopped and it didn't seem necessary to go into all this detail with strangers, however, now that John has seen all the schools and likes yours the best, it seems the thing to do, and you don't seem strangers any more.

Also to be considered must be Mr. Ford's feelings. They must be spared at any cost, he is so fine. He believes, and rightly so, that many boys on leaving college have to start learning the very things our boys here have the opportunity of learning as they go through school here. They work in any of the various departments of the Ford Motor Company all summer and half days in college, then when they graduate they can do some one thing well and have a knowledge of many others. The school here is one of Mr. Ford's "pets."

The pupils are chosen from among the employees, also residents of Dearborn. It is the "little brick schoolhouse" idea, the first and second grade in one school and third through seventh in another, with one teacher for each. In the High School there are many teachers but no languages are taught. However, many colleges do not require languages for entrance anymore. But it is the idea that John would like to get away and be prepared for anything. Also having been here all his life, it hasn't the glamour being around the Ford Motor Company has for others.

John may have to work with his hands later, who knows in this changing world of ours, but if he does, if he has also learned how to be happy, how to read a good book, how to make the best of things, he will never be lonely or too discouraged. He also feels that because of the course here, if he doesn't start somewhere else this year, it will be difficult for him to catch up, and he isn't one that likes to be behind.

I am so afraid that if you don't take him that another year he may not want to go, I feel that it is the psychological time right now. Having a very indulgent father, and being an only child, it has been rather hard for me to keep things sensible without being too stern a parent. You could help a lot if you would understand.

This thought occurred to me, I wonder if I could get someone in the town that you would know to board and room John so he could attend day school with you in the event you felt you couldn't crowd him in with your group.

The rest is up to you, you hold John's future in the palm of your hand. Please help.

Yours very truly,
(signed)

But even as her letter was winging its way to headmaster Boyden, his letter arrived:

My dear Mrs. Dallinger:

After your telephone call this morning I made a very careful survey of our enrollment situation, in the hope I might find some opening for your son, but I am sorry to report we are completely filled and I do not anticipate any withdrawals. I am very sorry for Mr. Allen gave me a good report about your boy.

If I can help you in any way with regard to some other school, please do not hesitate to let me know.

The next time you come east I hope you will stop at Deerfield and that I may have the pleasure of meeting you.

Cordially yours,
(signed)

So that settled the matter for the year. The fact that after all her efforts the headmaster had not even been impressed enough to get her name spelled right was most annoying. Of course, had Mr. Ford picked up the phone, I am sure I would have been in Deerfield immediately, but he was the last person we could go to for help, since he wanted me to stay where I was. So Mother did the next best thing: she sent a friendly note or two during the school term and then early the next spring got on the phone again to call headmaster Boyden.

Unfortunately, she was again afraid she had struck out, because she had reached him during his Sunday dinner. He still didn't think he had room for me.

Now she wrote a long letter to butter him up and show him her world and find a link between her world and his—a mutual love of horses (she eventually sent him one). The letter, of which I have the copy, is typed and reads:

Dear Mr. Boyden:

Mr. Allen told us you were quite a trotting horse fancier, our pacer won the Michigan three-year-old stake after we had tried twice before and always ran into some bad luck, such as distemper, etc., etc., you know the things that will happen to the best of cared for horses. We have a half-mile track here on the farm and Sundays, weather permitting, Mr. Dahlinger and I drive against each other.

You know I'm wondering if a letter I wrote you last October could have gone astray. I wrote then advising you that John would have no other school but yours, and asked about what subjects and books he would have had if he had been able to attend Deerfield. He wanted to know with the idea in mind he might keep up so as to be ready to enter this fall. I of course took it for granted you understood he would attend this fall. I had stated in my previous letters that yours was the only school he took to—the grounds and the atmosphere are a lot like Greenfield Village. I just can't tell him now you won't have him, he would be at loose ends, he's counted on it since last September, and I feel someway it must be my fault, I should have followed up my October letter, but when no answer came I presumed you thought it wasn't important enough to matter. John kept asking if I had heard from you, I told him "no, but was certain everything was all right," you can't let him down now.

Now Mr. Boyden, as one horse lover to another, couldn't you squeeze John in somewhere, I'm certain you wouldn't regret it.

If you ever come near Dearborn, please let us know, we would really show you some interesting things. That includes Mr. and Mrs. Allen also, they were so considerate when we were in Deerfield.

May I hear from you soon.

(signed)

I was one happy boy when I left home for Deerfield, and three years later, the summer that I was graduated, Mother showed her gratitude to Boyden by arranging to give the school a bus which it needed to carry the kids to sporting events. It was wartime and buses were impossible to get. I drove the thing myself from Dearborn to deliver it to the headmaster.

At the time of my arrival at school, I had no idea how poorly equipped I was. I knew no foreign language, so I had to be tutored in French, and my colleagues were ahead of me in every subject. Time and again, that first year, I wrote Mother that I was giving up, and she would phone or write me to hang on.

I had left Henry Ford with the impression that I wanted to be a doctor. This was a half-truth. The truth was I just wanted to get away from Ford and all things Ford. Miss Lynch was bugging me to be a doctor, and I did spend time in and around the Ford Hospital. I watched operations that were not too bloody, and they did not bother me too much.

When I got to Deerfield I still didn't know what I wanted to be, but it didn't matter; I was having enough trouble trying to catch up with the Eastern standards after going to the small Village school for nine years.

I found to my dismay that it was worse than I expected. I was behind by almost a year.

I think one letter shows it all—how Mother catered to me and never scolded about bad grades. No wonder I was a spoiled kid. Incidentally, the paint Mother is talking about would not be needed for at least a month because I didn't have the car with me.

May 21, 1940

Dear,

Here is the paint sample, also the leather—you see I haven't seen the blue leather 'til late last night, then waited 'til this a.m. for sunlight—this is the Zephyr Blue—We would have to go outside for the other blue and it would take too long now.

But in the meantime I will get busy and get other samples and we can do it over when you come home if you wish. It seems that US Royal cords can not be bought through Ford Motor Company—Mr. Edsel's orders—but Harold is going to find out today if we can't take a set of Firestones and trade with some US dealer and pay whatever necessary if you much prefer Royals—better let me know about that.

Someone, I've forgotten who it is, Firestone or Goodrich, make puncture proof tube of some kind. Do you know what I mean—or a blowout proof, perhaps. Would you like these? Now I remember, it is something about if you get a puncture, the tube stays up 'til you can get somewhere—besides in the ditch or else.

The Moreing show was quite the berries—The New York papers gave him a big write-up and so boosted the price of the pictures—I met some very interesting people. You would have loved it, and I would have been proud to have had you there.

Stayed 'til Saturday and really got a lot accomplished. Saw some very lovely rings, an estate was selling out.

I landed in New York at five minutes to four Monday and you would have died. There were only three other people besides myself in that big depot—my porter and two men who were cleaning the information booth. Seems there are no trains yet during those hours—I was awake on my train and so got up and went to the hotel. Would have had to get out of train at six o'clock anyway and by getting to hotel I got extra sleep. The car scored a piston at Indianapolis so hasn't qualified yet.

Everything about as usual. I thought you seemed a bit preoccupied when I was there. Hon, don't worry about your marks—better men than you have taken six or seven years to finish prep school, especially one as stiff as that—Love and understanding always,

Mom

My second year at Deerfield, I finally started to shape up a little, as a note from headmaster Boyden to Mother shows:

My dear Mrs. Dahlinger:

I am enclosing John's marks for the Winter term. On the whole they are better than in the fall, and I am confident now that he is willing to work.

Mr. Wickendon told me that he had a very long and satisfactory talk with you.

There is little I can add to what I told you the other day, except to say that I feel he has made real progress during the past three months.

I hope very much that you and Mr. Dahlinger will plan to come on for our Spring day on May 11th when most of the boys will have their parents here.

Cordially yours,
F. L. Boyden
(signed)

Incidentally, Gordon MacRae was a student at Deerfield at the same time I was. I remember he had a good voice even then, and he performed in the school's Gilbert and Sullivan productions.

When I was thirty and no longer the "Little Prince of Dearborn," I got nostalgic for old Deerfield and sent a note in my Christmas card to headmaster Boyden. Back came a letter within a few days:

Deerfield Academy
Deerfield, Massachusetts

December 28, 1953

Dear John:

Mrs. Boyden and I were very glad to receive your Christmas card for it recalls so many pleasant memories of the time when you were here and your father and mother used to visit us. I still have the sulky which your father sent to us and have just had to dispose of the bus which your mother made possible for us. I remember so well when you drove it in from Detroit. I don't know what we would have done without it all these years, and particularly during the war period when it was so difficult to get any transportation. It kept going until last spring when it really wasn't safe to drive any longer. It saved us thousands of dollars in transportation and also made possible many athletic contests with the neighboring schools.

I wrote to Mr. Ford thanking him for it when he was alive but presume he never saw the letter.

I hope things are going well with you and with all the family and I am sure you know how much we would like to have you stop by and see us. If we get out Detroit way we will hope to see you. A great many alumni have been coming in and it does seem good to see all the boys again.

Mrs. Boyden joins in sending best wishes to you and your father and mother for the New Year.

Cordially yours,
Frank L. Boyden
(signed)

Even though I had several tutors to help me put it together and catch up, my grades at first hovered in the almost flunking area of D. I was lucky to get through the three years with a C+ average.

Almost directly from the academy I volunteered for the navy. In fact, I would have gone immediately, but I was waiting for an old friend to finish Notre Dame so we could enlist together.

I was much more suited for military life than for the academy. I was suddenly getting grades between 3.7 and 3.8 as a naval air cadet. I had a good incentive. If I flunked officers' training school, I would become a swabby wearing bell bottoms, and I considered that the greatest possible punishment.

It was a great shot to my self-confidence to be a few points higher than my buddy in officer aptitude, though he would get slightly higher marks in certain scholastic subjects.

At first I had the best of all possible worlds. When I was stationed at flight preparatory school at Wooster, Ohio, I kept my own airplane—a Fairchild 24, registered in my Dad's name— at the local airport. Then the navy found out about it and decided it was against regulations.

I explained that I had my pilot's license, but they said it was the principle of the thing; I had to leave the plane in Dearborn. But since I was not confined to the base from Friday at six to taps on Sunday at ten, one of the Ford pilots would fly the Fairchild down, pick me up, and bring me back.

Just before World War II, I flew for Ford Motor Company. I would fly to Willow Run and back again. One particular time I almost didn't make it. They had overloaded my light plane with blueprints and other things. I skimmed over the trees and barely missed landing on top of the Dearborn Inn.

Because of my civilian flying, I was sent to the Atlanta advanced instrument training school base. After completing my tour in Atlanta, I was assigned to Pensacola. I had two weeks' leave between the time I was commissioned and the time I assumed duties as an ensign, and Ford sent their twin-engine Beach plane down to bring me home for my two-week leave.

Things at home were not the same. The war had completely changed Ford Motor Company. There had been a mad scramble to build the Willow Run bomber plant and to convert the Rouge from automobiles to military vehicles. Dad was in charge of clearing the land and readying the site for the construction of the bomber plant.

At Pensacola I progressed to the navy's highest instrument rating, with the green card which allowed a pilot to file his own instrument clearance. In the army you had to have the rank of captain to qualify for a green card, plus the same minimum of 2,000 hours.

It came to pass on one instrument flight from Pensacola to Atlanta that we ran into some thunderstorms on the trip up. Although no difficulty resulted, on my return flight, when I filed my clearance, it was turned down by the weather officer, who happened to be a colonel. I asked what was wrong; he said he felt the weather was too severe to fly through.

I said, "I came through it earlier, and I don't feel it's any problem."

He said, "I cannot sign your clearance."

I said, "I can. And I will." And I did, and he damn near had a heart attack, because I was only an ensign. I produced my green card, and he almost had a second heart attack. What he didn't know was that I had already had over 2,000 hours flight time before I entered the service.

I taught at Pensacola all through the war. I was ready to ship out about the time of V-J day. But by then I had enough points to get out of service. If there had been a jet, I would have been on it.

I enlisted in the navy late in 1942 and got out in time for deer hunting: November 17, 1945. I drove home, because by then, being an officer, I had a car—you can bet it was a Ford.

Every now and then it came in handy to have a Ford connection. The executive officer was having trouble with his car. Due to war shortages, he couldn't get parts. I arranged with Dad to have a new engine shipped down to the Ford dealer in Pensacola to be installed in his car. Needless to say, I was a hero on that one.

When I was stationed at Iowa City for a while, I accidentally ran into the doctor who had delivered me at Ford Hospital— Dr. Plass. With all the babies he had delivered, he still reacted strongly as soon as he heard the name John Dahlinger. He immediately invited me to his house and was extremely friendly.

That was the good part at Iowa. The bad part was the physical fitness program. It was under Minnesota's famous football coach Bernie Bierman, whom most of the cadets considered a sadist. The obstacle course was so brutal that my buddy from Notre Dame frequently would throw up, not once but two times, before completing it in the fifteen to twenty minutes allowed.

It was a relief to get away from there and go to Minneapolis for primary training in the larger planes. We had been flying Piper cubs; now we flew Stearmans.

The good thing about Minneapolis was its man-hungry women. The only males seemed to be those at a camp for retired army personnel and a training camp for Japanese-Americans. Honeywell and other war plants were almost completely staffed with women who were ready and willing to take a man to dinner before some other woman got hold of him. The cadets never had it so good.

On the other hand, the bad news was that we were stationed there in winter, and the Stearman was an open-cockpit plane. It was colder than hell, and there was no heater in those turkeys.

When it came to uniforms I added a touch of class by ignoring the navy store and ordering mine from Mr. Ford's and Dad's tailor. Whenever I was home on leave I just had him make up the blues, the tans, and the grays. The navy was using a drab shade of gray. I picked out a much better shade and got away with it—it was close enough.

Mr. Ford put the finishing touch to my image by getting me solid gold wings. And my mother gave me my gold navy ring. I still treasure them. Ford kept reminding me there was a place for me in his company.

I remember Mr. Ford telling me at that time, "You can write

your own ticket, John. You could do a lot here. I'd back you up." I explained that there was still a war on and I had my job *there* before I could think of anything else.

When the war ended I was still an ensign. Most of my time had been spent going through cadet training. By now everything was really different at Ford Motor Company—Henry II had taken over. I still wasn't ready to go to work at Ford. I wanted something really exciting, and I found it in racing cars.

We had three midget Offy race cars which Dad had bought from Ronnie Householder, the famous race driver, when Ronnie went into the service. Dad had some spare parts in his racing stable, enough to construct a fourth car. In 1946, at the age of twenty-three, I went on the racing circuit and managed a team.

At first I did a little racing myself, until word got back to Dearborn and the folks threatened to take back their cars if I raced again. I will admit that racing was a fairly bloody sport; even at my first Indy race, three people were killed in my sight. Ours was quite a grueling schedule—we'd race seven days a week, twice on Sundays.

I'd know it was Sunday if we were in Sharon, Pennsylvania. From there we'd load up and rush to Cleveland Sportsman Park for Sunday-night racing under the lights. We won the Michigan-Ohio Point Championship two years in a row.

We finally cut down to six days; you can't work on cars and sleep at the same time. I can still remember the schedule: Monday resting or racing in Detroit; Tuesday in Toledo; Wednesday, Akron; Thursday, Detroit; Friday, Canfield, Ohio; Saturday, Toledo; and Sunday, back in Sharon and Cleveland.

I could only take a couple of years of it. Besides, after several years, racing was reaching the saturation point, and I had to spend too much money to stay competitive. At any race there would be sixty or seventy cars showing up, and only twenty could qualify.

Soon I was representing a steel forging company out of Alliance, Ohio—Transue and Williams Steel Forging Company. I was responsible for supplying the Ford Motor Company from

1949 until the early fifties. Then, with Mrs. Ford dead and Dad swept out of the company, the rug was also pulled from under me. Ford Motor Company set up its own forging operation, and there was very little I could supply the Ford Motor Company.

Ford purchased a forging plant of its own in Canton, Ohio, so actually I was competing with the factory itself; they were taking the good stuff, and we were getting cats and dogs. Their goal was not to spite me, perhaps, but they were sure putting me out of business.

I still wasn't ready to sit down at a desk. So I purchased a supper club called Cliff Bell's in downtown Detroit, in a good location where all the hotels were. I featured fine food and entertainment.

My first wedding took place on a very unfortunate day—the anniversary of Henry Ford's death, April 7, 1956. We damn near divorced on the honeymoon. But we didn't, and one son was born of this marriage. He is now twenty-one and lives with his mother. She and I split in 1957, but it took several years to get the decree. Again, it was that awful month of April, in 1961.

The next time I married in October—of the same year, 1961.

Together Bette and I planned a new supper club, Act IV. It was well named, because we were right across from the Fisher Theater, where all the live plays were performed. But I'm sure that Henry Ford must have turned over in his grave to know that I not only was smoking but was trafficking in alcoholic spirits. But he would have been pleased to know I chose Walter Buhl Ford, the husband of my old playmate, Dody Ford, to do the renovation. Josephine Ford came to see the job her husband had done in converting the office building that I had taken over. She seemed quite impressed with Act IV, but did not seem inclined to talk about old times when we fellows had let her be the only girl in our tree house, so I did not reminisce.

Just about everybody in show business who passed through Detroit either performed at our supper club or was a guest there.

Among the performers at our club were Mel Tormé, Myron
Cohen, Buddy Greco, John Davidson, Pete Barbuti, Kay Bal-
lard, Kay Stevens, Joan Rivers, Dick Cavett, George Carlin,
Rodney Dangerfield, Jackie Mason, Louis Nye, and Johnny
Desmond. The place was a hangout for those who were appear-
ing at Fisher Theater across the street and other spots around
town—Buddy Hackett, Robert Goulet, Shirley Jones and Jack
Cassidy, Ethel Merman, Dame Judith Anderson, Henry Man-
cini, Mitzi Gaynor, Jack Carter, Gordon and Sheila MacRae,
Shirley Eder, and Billy Daniels.

Act IV was a great success from the day it opened in October
1963 until the riots in the summer of 1967 wrecked midtown
Detroit. I sold the club in January 1969 and wondered what to
do next. Someone had me halfway interested in a banana plan-
tation, and there were several other exotic offers, but my
mother's poor health changed everything.

When she became so weak that I had to manage her affairs,
I began to read for the first time all the papers and diaries and
notes and legal papers she had kept well hidden from me all
through the years.

I became so fascinated that I decided to take a little time to
really get acquainted with the man who most probably was my
father.

I was not the only one delving into the past of Mother and
Henry Ford. Professor David L. Lewis of the University of
Michigan was also on the trail of Mrs. D. He came to the door of
our summer home; the housekeeper refused him entrance and
permission to photograph the property.

Lewis then wrote the housekeeper asking if he could meet
with Mrs. D. The letter didn't reach my hands right away; when
it did, I decided to let sleeping dogs lie.

When Lewis's book came out in 1976, I got a copy and naturally looked for Dad's and Mother's names. The only one listed
in the index was Mr. D., with only one page reference. I said to
myself: After forty-four years with Ford, is that all there is?

And then, when I read the lonely reference, I was further distressed to see that it was incorrect. It said that the day Ford died he visited Ray Dahlinger's "former" office.

This led to my calling him. I wanted Dr. Lewis to know that Ray Dahlinger had still been employed by the company at the time of Ford's death, and for three years thereafter.

Lewis acknowledged the error and said, "That will have to be corrected." We had a friendly conversation in which he said that from what he could see, Mr. D. was one of the "unsung heroes" of the Ford Motor Company and that Mother deserved to be acknowledged for the work she had done in helping to construct Greenfield Village. I promised to let Dr. Lewis know when I could see him, as he was eager to meet me. Perhaps now he will understand why I didn't call again. I still was not interested in divulging intimate family matters.

Sometime after that phone conversation, as I thumbed through his book, something caught my eye in the introduction: Lewis's assertion that there was circumstantial evidence of a brief and intense extramarital affair that Ford had had in the early 1920s.

I had kept quiet all through the years, but here was a respected professor practically putting it on the line. For the Detroit-Dearborn crowd, he might just as well have named names. He could only mean me, born in April 1923.

I suddenly felt that the time had come to say what needed to be said, to clear the air and have done with it, especially since the Ford family and Ford Museum had done such a good job of obviously excluding all evidence of Evangeline and Ray Dahlinger.

I went to the museum and searched in vain for identification tags that would mention the Dahlingers. I looked in indexes of numerous books and found practically no mention of us.

I found it particularly odd that in the several books I read about Ford and Ford Motor Company little or nothing was said about Mother or Dad and their influence and position at Ford Motor Company. Nor was anything said about the close friendship existing between Mr. Ford and Mother and Dad.

It seems to me that their names may have been purposely expunged from the Ford Archives for reasons unknown. Actually, I can guess at reasons why this would be done, but I think the Dahlinger name only became conspicuous by its absence. Then when later writers went to the Ford Archives for material, they found only a few disparaging references to us. Any mention is a put-down, or makes it seem that the Dahlingers were of the servant class.

At best Mother is called some kind of social secretary. Mr. and Mrs. D. may have started in relatively humble positions, but they certainly were not servants, and they rose to top-level rank in the Ford Company, which is never acknowledged in anything I have read.

As a matter of fact, Mother was the first top female executive at Ford and the only female executive there in her time. I would not even say we lived in the upper middle class—it was much better than that. We lived an élite and privileged life in which money was no object. My parents were a privy council to Mr. Ford.

What is very telling is that Professor Lewis has stated that he spent nineteen years researching Ford and going through the Ford Archives for *The Public Image of Henry Ford*. Evidently he found next to nothing there about the Dahlingers. Yet, probably in conversations with old-timers, he found enough arrows pointing to us that he decided to come, camera in hand, to our house to investigate further.

Nevins and Hill, in *Ford* (Vol. 3: *Decline and Rebirth*), wrote that Dad had done a lousy job building the auto test track at the Ford Airport. The authors' exact words were:

> Built under the inexpert direction of Dahlinger, it was a rudimentary affair, with stretches of dry asphalt, wet asphalt, and standing water which eventually the Engineering Department would have to rebuild.

I'd like to say a word in Dad's defense. The test track was put where it was because Henry Ford wanted it that way. There were very few planes coming in, and Mr. Ford wanted to make use of some of the runways. When a plane was coming in, the pilot would notify the field, an alarm would sound, and the test drivers would scurry off the test track. This was the first test track at Ford, and everyone got a little smarter when they were building the second one.

Other than Lewis's inaccurate reference and the little slap at Dad's ability in a book by Nevins and Hill, there was almost nothing about Dad.

I am glad I have finally found my own voice and decided to break the seeming conspiracy of silence. Otherwise the record would be blank forever and the history of Ford would indeed be *bunk*.

14

The Tragedy
of Edsel Ford

I'm glad I was raised as Ray Dahlinger's son. I would hate to have been treated the way Edsel was.

From Mother and Dad I heard many times about the terrible situation that existed between Henry Ford and his son. Edsel Ford was thirty years old when I was born. As I became conscious of the people around me, I thought of him at first only as the father of my playmates Henry, Ben, Dody, and Billy.

It was only years later that I realized he was, in all probability, my half-brother. It was uncanny how much alike we looked. Henry Ford made a few references to Mother about it, not realizing it would mean anything to me, and at the time it didn't. But when you hear that you look more like somebody every day and that you look like someone used to look, you do start to pay attention to how that person looks.

Edsel Ford was a good man to resemble, because he was very slim and very good looking. I was slightly taller than Edsel, about the same height as Mr. Ford. A picture taken of me when I was at a boating party happens to have been shot from the same angle as a picture taken of Edsel at about the same age. We do look quite alike. But in disposition we were quite different. I was more like Mr. Ford—tough. Edsel was the gentlest man I ever knew, and perhaps the kindest.

I must have looked a lot more like Henry Ford as a child than his grandchildren did, because he chose me to pose for paintings of him as a youngster which were being executed by Irving R. Bacon. I was less than thrilled to have to sit long hours when I was twelve years old, while the painter worked at depicting Ford as a young mechanical genius.

As Mr. Ford said to Mother, in his typically understated way, "Well, John will do. It's close enough. It's close enough."

I was so used to being chosen for things that I didn't attach much importance to it, but Ford did say to Mother, "Henry and Benson don't look anything like me, and Billy is too young. John looks more like me than any of them."

Edsel was already president of the Ford Motor Company when I was born. Ford had given him the post five years before, in December 1918, when he was only twenty-five.

Edsel's tragedy was that he could not stand up to his father. He was too much like his mother and could not stand turmoil and dissension, which was what Henry Ford thrived on. When Edsel was upset about what his father had said or done to undermine him, he would throw up.

I have often tried to figure out how Edsel might have managed his father better. I know that simply giving in on every point and making excuses for his father to others was not the answer.

I know that I got along much better with Mr. Ford by being stubborn and independent and arguing a lot until he gave in or forgot about it. There was hardly a way that Mr. Ford did not show his irritation with Edsel, and yet Edsel maintained a martyr's smile.

Mother was always coming home with some story of Mr.

Ford's "dirty trick." The fact that they usually cost the company money meant nothing to Ford when he wanted to teach his son a lesson. I remember an incident that would be very funny if it weren't also a little sad.

Edsel had hired a decorator to design a nice office for him in the Rouge administration building at Dearborn, to which the Ford hierarchy had moved from Highland Park. He was so pleased with the results that he wanted his father to have an equally nice office near his, and he kept the decorator on to do the job.

When Mr. Ford came to see his new office, he picked one item to go into a rage over—a beautiful marble fireplace. Edsel stood by and suffered as his father ordered the thing torn out immediately. Mr. Ford had plain brick installed instead.

Now it was the decorator's turn to be furious. Naturally she directed her anger at Edsel, who was supposedly in charge. Edsel, who lacked the heart to stand up to an angry father or an angry woman, again gave in. He stood by helplessly as the decorator had the brick torn back out and the marble reinstalled.

Mr. Ford took one look, Mother said, and never used that office again; instead, he would use other people's offices. But he also had another office at the engineering lab.

There was a period when Mother became Edsel's spy. They were the same age, born within a few months of each other in 1893. She would tip Edsel off on some dirty trick that Mr. Ford was going to play on him. Sometimes she would know of Mr. Ford's plans from what Ford himself had told her, so she would have to be careful that she didn't appear disloyal.

Sometimes she would squeeze the information out of Dad; other times he would tell her something casually. Dad had no idea she was passing the information on to Edsel, or it would have hit the fan. Dad was more loyal to Ford, in this way, than she was.

But Mother had humanity on her side. She said she couldn't stand to see the Boss abuse his son that way.

I have often wondered whether Edsel saw or knew something

about Mother and Ford, and whether this contributed to the bad feeling between father and son. Surely, with all that talk going around, Edsel must have known or heard something about the relationship. He was no dummy.

Mother and Edsel had a special rapport, a common respect and understanding. She even had a code name with Mr. Edsel. When she would call him at his office or at home to warn him of some dirty business underfoot, she used the name Mrs. Grey.

I'm sure Mrs. Edsel knew who Mrs. Grey was, but the servants never did, and I doubt very much if his personal secretary knew. Mr. Edsel knew when he heard Mrs. Grey was calling that the fat was in the fire, and he would take the call.

I remember one time she called him at their summer home in Bar Harbor, Maine, shortly before he was supposed to return home, and perhaps prevented his stepping into a trap that had been baited for his arrival.

She was very careful about calling him at the plant because of the possibility of Bennett's having planted a spy. I'm sure she didn't cure all the problems he had with his father, but she at least helped to soften some of the blows.

Mrs. Ford had to be a Minnie Mouse to allow Mr. Ford to do the things he did to Edsel. My mother would never have allowed Mr. D. to do to me what Mr. Ford did to Edsel. From Mother I knew that Edsel did not go to his mother for sympathy. He did not tell her how terrible it was for him. He did not want Mrs. Ford to worry.

I could see even as a child that Mrs. Ford was very docile with the Boss, and he was in complete charge. He was polite rather than courtly to her.

If Mrs. Ford pumped me about Mother, I hardly realized it; but I knew she seemed to be very aware of her.

Edsel had two strikes against him from the start: Henry Ford was his father, and, secondly, he was born without a certain kind of acid in his system.

At the time, I didn't pay too much attention when Lynchy explained about the deficiency, but it was a very serious matter.

As a boy Edsel had an unfortunate experience that may have

prompted his father to start losing confidence in him. Ford had let Edsel work in a home workshop, and Edsel lost the tip of his finger using one of the power tools. Mother said Mr. Ford was bitterly disappointed that Edsel was not as mechanically inclined as he.

I was not much of a scholar, but I certainly had a mechanical aptitude, and this gave Mr. Ford and me many happy hours together.

According to one story I heard, Mr. Ford even ignored Christmas when Edsel was a little boy. It wasn't the happiest time for a little child whose daddy did not have time to get him a Christmas tree.

I was lucky to have come late in Mr. Ford's life, when he had time to spend. I guess I got some of the time that Edsel never had lavished on him. I remember that up in Ford's private workshop, above his garage, we would tinker with watches; I was permitted to take one apart as Ford watched and assisted. He was my helper; he let me be boss.

Edsel, too, had tried to work with his father in their workshop in the old house in Detroit. But that was very grim and earnest work, and Mr. Ford gave all the orders. Edsel's tragedy was that Henry Ford never let Edsel be the boss!

You would think Edsel was working for someone else, the way his father ordered men to spy on him. If they didn't, they were in danger of being fired. When I was being carefully guarded for security reasons because of union threats, all of Edsel Ford's children were being guarded too.

I don't know whether Mr. Ford used my guard as a way to keep tabs on Mother, but I do know from her that he used the Edsel guards to keep tabs on Edsel. In fact, he slipped them a little extra money sometimes.

At any rate, Henry Ford knew almost every trivial thing that Edsel was doing, and now and then at our house he would complain about Edsel and how there seemed no way to toughen him up. "The boy is soft," he would say. "Everybody leads him."

What he was really angry about was that Edsel seemed to respect other people's views as much as his father's—and sometimes more. Usually sons are victims of overly intense mothers. But instead of "smother-love," Edsel was the victim of some kind of twisted father love.

If someone became Edsel's friend and tried to influence him in any way, Mr. Ford was fiendish about breaking it up. He would deride the fellow to Edsel, and he would even try to turn the friend against Edsel, with his "he's no friend of yours" trick.

Henry Ford would do all kinds of things to humiliate his son in front of company officials. He once asked him at a business meeting whether the books were all in balance. Edsel, at a nod from his accountants, said of course they were.

This was just the opening Ford was looking for. He had been, unknown to Edsel, renovating a yacht.

"Oh, they are?" sneered Henry. "You don't know anything that's going on, and you're surrounded by crooks."

"What do you mean, Dad?" stammered Edsel, touching his sensitive stomach.

"There has just been a half-million-dollar expenditure on re-building a yacht—someone around here is a crook."

It was one of the few times Edsel talked back, but even then his voice was soft rather than sharp. "Well, in that case," said Edsel, almost surprised at his own daring, "the crook would have to be you."

One of the meanest things Henry Ford did was to force Edsel to get rid of his brother-in-law, Ernest Kanzler. Kanzler's only crime was to be married to the sister of Eleanor Ford, Edsel's wife. I should say his real crime was to have become Edsel's friend, and to have allowed Edsel to lean on him a little too much—at the Ford plant and after hours.

Kanzler was one of the titleless executives of the Ford Company; nepotism was a way of life at Ford. For that matter, Henry Ford's own wife had gotten one of her relatives on the payroll, too, a fellow named George Brubaker.

But George Brubaker was smart enough not to try to be close to Edsel.

Ford tried to keep his executives from building homes in Grosse Pointe, and he would not hire anyone who came from that "phony" place. Edsel had infuriated his father by building a home there after he married the woman he loved, Eleanor Clay. The fact that many of the best people of Detroit moved to Grosse Pointe only meant, to Ford, that they were "social climbers." If memory serves, Edsel's house may even have been built on land that Henry Ford himself had purchased in the Grosse Pointe area before he became disenchanted with the place. It would not be impossible. It would have been typical Ford inconsistency.

If Ford could have driven Edsel out of Grosse Pointe, he would have. But Edsel was married to a very strong and brave woman who stood up to Henry Ford. Even so, as Mother learned, Henry Ford had had the effrontery to invade Eleanor Ford's domain in Edsel's absence and break all his liquor bottles. Ford had decided that Edsel's delicate stomach and stomach pains were nothing but hangovers from too much liquor. Until the very end, Ford refused to believe that his son could have stomach cancer. He called it undulant fever, appendicitis, and everything but.

As I understand it, Edsel first had an ulcer. And had the ulcer been taken care of sooner, it might not have developed into cancer.

When Mr. Ford would really blow up at his son, Edsel would stay away a few days and get heavily into the sauce. This, of course, did not help his stomach.

I do not know what effect being born without that acid in his system had on Edsel's later health, but it would perhaps indicate that his stomach might have been a sensitive area under pressure—and Edsel certainly lived under pressure.

Edsel was not an alcoholic, but I think he did drink to help deaden the emotional pain his father inflicted on him. But even when distressed he did not blame his father, who seemed so heartless.

Edsel found his greatest joy in art. He was very fond of

great works of art. This is probably what goaded Ford into saying, "I wouldn't give five cents for all the finest art in the world." Edsel had a lot of fine paintings and sculptures in his Grosse Pointe home, and Ford was very unimpressed with them.

Mr. Ford was not really even very interested in the exterior beauty of his early automobiles. Only because the competition was making inroads into sales did he finally decide he had better compete on a car's outside appearance as well as its performance.

I too was very interested in art at an early age, but it was nothing that anyone took very seriously. Fortunately it tended mostly to the drawing of cars and planes. My interest in art was inspired by the fact that I had my first crush on my art teacher, Miss Coe, who later married the athletic director and swimming coach of Greenfield Village School, Dall Hutchinson.

Some said that Edsel could have been a great artist if he hadn't been born a Ford. He dabbled in sculpture, but more important was his contribution as a patron of the arts. He is the one who gave the Diego Rivera frescoes to the Detroit Institute of Arts. And he probably saved the institute by reaching into his own pocket to pay salaries during the Great Depression.

Henry Ford was not the only Ford with a flair for publicity. Edsel had one too, when it came to the Art Institute. He once got Admiral Byrd to lecture on his second Antarctic expedition in order to raise funds for the Institute. Edsel had the plane in which Byrd had flown on his first expedition set up in the middle of a street in Detroit—Washington Boulevard—with its wings filling the whole avenue.

So many people flocked to see the plane that had been named for my childhood playmate, Dody—the *Josephine Ford*—that a lot of money was made in the interest of art.

Edsel was very interested in safe driving programs for youngsters, and he set up the Ford Good Drivers League, which years later served as a guide in teaching driving in high schools across the country.

Another thing he did for kids was to reward those who built the best model airplanes by giving them free trips to Washington in a Ford trimotor plane. This was before I was old enough to participate, but I heard all about how those winners were invited to the White House to fly their planes, with Calvin Coolidge looking on. I believe that President Herbert Hoover also presided over these programs.

Edsel lived at 1100 Lakeshore Drive. His estate was situated right on Lake St. Clair, and it even had its own lovely private lagoon. It was fashioned after a Cotswold cottage, or rather a tremendous group of them linked together.

Edsel's home was really beautiful, reflecting his interest in art. He and Eleanor went to England several times to study architecture, and then they hired the famous architect Albert Kahn to design their place.

I thought Edsel had a much grander place than his father, and maybe this is one more thing that galled Mr. Ford. Edsel had sixty-five acres of beautifully landscaped lawns and gardens, a 132′ x 40′ swimming pool, and all kinds of buildings. The kids had their own playhouse, for example; and besides the sixty-room main house, there was the gate house, the boathouse, the greenhouse, the recreation house, and a kennel. And of course room for many cars—twenty or thirty—in the garages.

Naturally, Edsel Ford was a car buff. He had European and American cars, including, of course, the more luxurious Ford products, Mercury and Lincoln. He would drive competitors' cars around to make a comparison—I recall Studebakers and Packards.

For himself, Edsel liked prestige cars. Henry Ford always drove the humble man's car, except that on the inside, with all the additional fittings, it wasn't so humble anymore.

I would inherit some of Edsel's cars. After Edsel had played around with them and the company had thoroughly tested them, I'd usually keep them for a time.

The one in the museum now which is still on the Bugatti list is still in Edsel's name, but I used it after he did. It was made in

France by Italian manufacturers. Some $50,000 or $60,000 replicas of the Bugatti Royale are now being made. It was a car of the '20s—I believe a 193, Type 37 sports car of the 1926–30 era.

The MG I drove is in the Ford Museum too. So is the Citroën. Also the Cord, which was an American car nicknamed the "coffin nose."

Not enough is said, I think, about the fact that Edsel Ford was the one who gave the ultimate touch of class to the line of Ford automobiles. That was the Lincoln Continental, and Edsel created it with the help of Eugene Gregorie and coach builder Raymond H. Dietrich. They worked together to give birth to this classic beauty. Edsel had good taste and appreciated simple, sweeping lines.

I don't believe Henry Ford ever truly appreciated its beauty.

Edsel was unlike his father in another respect as well. Once one was working for Ford, Mr. Ford bitterly resented his doing anything else for another auto company. But when Dietrich had a chance to design an automobile for Packard Company and checked it out with Edsel first, Edsel not only gave his approval, but encouraged Dietrich to expand in his career.

Perhaps one reason Henry Ford was so against putting Ford stock on the open market was that Edsel came up with the idea first and for a time tried to sell Mr. Ford on it. He reasoned that if the company had a million shareholders and a board of directors representing people who were not of the Ford family, everything would be run in a more businesslike way.

And it certainly would have taken the heat off Edsel. But Ford liked things just the way they were. He liked having a son who was president of the company and whom he could order around as if he himself were still president.

Everyone around the plant, except Edsel, was amused by the way Ford would not go to Edsel's office, but would stop at someone else's office—Dad's or Harry Bennett's, for example—and summon Edsel to come there. The president of the Ford

Motor Company had to run to meet his father as if he were an office boy.

But whatever was thrown at him, and whatever it did to his delicate stomach, Edsel took it in good grace.

I don't think I ever heard Edsel raise his voice, though I hear he did on a few very rare occasions. You didn't have to ask him to repeat something, but his voice was so soft that you might have to lean forward a little, or at least pay close attention, to hear him.

Edsel was totally unlike his father in his attitude toward minorities. When two of his sons came to work at summer jobs, they were put in the engineering department, under a black employee.

Harry Bennett more or less reflected Henry Ford's attitude. Getting quite excited, he suggested the boys be moved to work under a white person, but Edsel would have none of it. He said it was good for the boys to learn to work with Negroes as well as whites.

The inside story of Edsel's illness was that the ulcers had turned cancerous from neglect, according to Miss Lynch, and even when Edsel was ready for an operation, it was put off because of the head surgeon's illness.

According to Lynchy, nobody wanted to touch Edsel at the hospital because they all knew it would be an unsuccessful operation. Someone from outside the hospital finally operated, in the absence of head surgeon McClure.

As for Ford's persistent claim that Edsel died of undulant fever, his own logic left him when he made that claim. We all drank the same milk from the Ford farms, and if he got it, it stands to reason that at least one or two other people would have contracted it too. But no one ever did.

Later, in keeping with Ford's belief in reincarnation, he sometimes said that Edsel was not really dead.

I knew a year in advance that Edsel was dying, because Lynchy knew it through her hospital connections. But I did not talk about it to anyone except Mother and Dad. I think the only ones around Edsel and Henry Ford who didn't know that Edsel was dying were Edsel and Mr. Ford.

After Edsel died in April 1943, some of these childish tricks must have come back to haunt Mr. Ford—like the time he watched Edsel get a coke oven built and then had it torn down.

But maybe the most embarrassing thing Henry Ford did was to go over Edsel's head to start rival Ford dealerships across the street from existing Ford dealerships. Henry Ford felt he had been abused when he had spot-checked a dealership some distance from Detroit.

Unfortunately, Dad was not driving him that day, or he might have been able to alert the proprietors to the fact that they had a distinguished guest. They did not recognize Henry Ford's visage and treated him like plain folks. Even worse, they were in a foul mood and reluctant to serve him.

Mr. Ford was still fuming at their abusive treatment years afterward, when he commented on how he had fixed them by ordering another dealership directly across the street "to shake them up a little." He liked the idea so much he ordered it done at random across the country.

The scream was heard all the way to Edsel's office as Henry Ford's trusted lieutenant rushed around buying land and getting the competition started. Edsel had to take a lot of abuse from outraged agency men until he prevailed on his father, through go-betweens, to call off this internecine war.

Edsel, Mother said, wanted to quit many times. He could have, because any number of companies wanted him to serve as a full-time director, and had they known he was available they would have jumped to get him, if only to learn how to compete with Ford. But Edsel's loyalty was such that he would end up telling Mother or one of the men, "Well, that's just Dad," or "Well, it's Dad's company, so I guess he can do what he wants with it."

The things that happened to Edsel shouldn't have happened to a dog. In fact, it's a good analogy, because, like a dog, he lost his best friend when Mr. Ford fired Edsel's assistant and confidant, John Crawford.

Again, the man's only crime was that he cared deeply for his boss, Edsel, and tried to protect him and advise him—which was what he was being paid for, anyway. But Ford was up to his old tricks, suggesting to various Ford officials that they fire John Crawford because he was "not good for Edsel." He said Crawford kept Edsel's stomach in an uproar.

The fact that Ford thought that men with lower rank in the company could fire the president's assistant was in itself an affront to Edsel. They begged off. Finally Ford told a man who had been with him almost the longest to do the firing. That was Charlie Sorensen, who was the working head of the company and as tough a man as Ford—if not tougher.

Ford told Sorensen, "He's making Edsel sick, and I don't want to see him around here." Very quickly Crawford was gone. Mother said that, again, Edsel was thinking of leaving the company. The Crawford case was typical of Ford's jealousy of anyone who was close to Edsel.

Another quaint trick of old Mr. Ford's, guaranteed to upset Edsel, was to call his son for his opinion on some matter, pretend he was going to take his advice, and then do the opposite.

It wasn't just in big decisions about the running of the plant, or the kind of cars to make, or changes in sales techniques; it could be about the most trivial things. But whatever it was, it would leave Edsel with egg on his face. Once it concerned whether Ford should go on the air to urge people to stand behind President Franklin Delano Roosevelt in the preparedness program before World War II.

This was about 1940 or early '41, and war clouds had been gathering. Henry Ford had indeed been thinking about American defense and was making plans for production of hundreds of thousands of bomber planes.

So there was nothing wrong with the idea of Ford's going on the radio to urge the public to support the president. He didn't need Edsel Ford to tell him what to do. However, he said that his aides had better get Edsel on the phone so he could check with him, and if Edsel said it was all right, he would do it.

They should have smelled a skunk right then. Edsel, who was a personal friend of FDR, of course urged him to go ahead. And Ford pretended he was going along with it.

Elaborate preparations were made to wire up an office in which Ford would speak. Then he just backed out as we knew he would, since Edsel would be left holding the microphone, so to speak. I was always so sorry that Edsel was not a fighter. If he had just yelled at his father or showed anger, I think Ford would have respected him. But as it was, Ford had little regard for him because he would not stand and fight.

Edsel hated confrontations of any kind. I heard that once, when a bunch of union men were coming, he simply left his office. They wouldn't believe he wasn't there, and before security could be called to get them out, they stormed Edsel's office and jumped around on his furniture. One angry man stomped on Edsel's desk with his shoes, scratching it up.

When I was ten, in 1933, Mr. Ford was seventy, which seemed very old to me. He was in excellent physical shape, and he remained so until he had a slight stroke in 1939. He was seventy-six, and I was sixteen. But he was completely recovered within a few months.

I think he felt better than ever. He square-danced as usual, and he could dance the pants off most of the younger men. And he continued to relish his life and his high position and his tormenting of Edsel.

In 1941 Henry Ford had a second stroke, from which he seemed to recover.

But then in 1943 everything came to a screeching halt when Edsel died. And it really had been stomach cancer and not undulant fever. There had been fever, but it had been caused by the cancer. But some of the papers still printed that Edsel had died of undulant fever.

Ford never believed that Edsel had had incurable stomach

cancer. He still said his son could have been saved if only Dr. McClure, head surgeon of Ford Hospital, had done the operating.

After Edsel died, Mr. Ford never danced again. From 1943 until he died, he was never really the same. Even so, Henry Ford took over the helm again, becoming president for a second time at Ford Motor Company.

Eleanor Ford, Edsel's widow, was a tougher customer to deal with than her husband had been. Even as poor Ford grieved for his son, understanding, I think, at last how he had failed him, and secretly swallowing the bitterness of his guilt, Eleanor slapped him with a new demand—that Henry II be made vice-president.

To accomplish this, young Henry had to be released from the navy. An appeal was quietly made to President Roosevelt, Edsel's old friend, and FDR himself gave the discharge order.

The second step in this power play, which occurred two years later, in 1945, was one that the ladies of the family had learned from Mr. Ford himself. Clara Ford and Eleanor Ford cornered Ford. With Clara to back her up, Eleanor threatened to put her share of the family stock—about a third of the stock of the company—on the open market unless Ford stepped down and made Henry II the full president of the company. Up against the wall, with Eleanor and Clara working as a team, Mr. Ford grudgingly gave in.

But it was not the old warrior who had given in. All the fight had gone from him with the death of Edsel.

I was in the service when Henry II took over the company— September 20, 1945—and as his first order of business fired Bennett. The sighs of relief and shouts of joy were so loud that I could practically hear them several hundred miles away. We all knew what was going on at Ford Motor Company with the Bennett regime. There had to be a house cleaning. It probably should have happened sooner than it did. Had I been in Henry II's shoes I would have done the same—at that point in time there was no alternative. Henry had inherited enough toughness from his grandfather to do a hell of a good job reorganizing a *new* Ford Motor Company.

Actually, it was all done in very good form, and Bennett was permitted to retire. He was kept on the payroll for some time, but his power was gone and he knew it and never showed his face around the plant again. He moved to California.

Now and then, in his last days, Henry Ford would forget that Harry Bennett was gone and would ask Dad to drive him over to Harry's office.

After Bennett left, many stories circulated about how afraid Ford executives had been of him. He was the most powerful man around the company and had tried to replace Ford men with his own people. If Henry II had not fired him, it's hard to say what the future of the company would have been.

After 1945, Mr. Ford was a pathetic figure. Toward the end, starting in 1946, Mother was really worried, because Ford was not himself anymore. He was on pills—Phenobarbitals and Seconals. This we know because Mother, who was greatly concerned, obtained a few of his pills and had Miss Lynch take them to Ford Hospital for identification. His second stroke had actually weakened him greatly.

By now his reliance was all on Dad. Almost every day, he'd say where he wanted to go and Dad would take him driving. The day he died, he visited Dad, which was most unusual. Usually Dad went to him.

The end came unexpectedly on April 7, 1947. It had been raining so heavily that the Ford private power plant (Ford had his own generator for his estate) had been flooded and the electricity was out. In fact, the reason he had come to get Dad was to see if they couldn't get it running again. They did for a little while, and Ford was rather proud of the fact that they didn't have to send for anyone to do it. But then it stopped again.

Still the rains came. Mother worried that Ford would catch cold from having gone out to get Dad.

The Tragedy of Edsel Ford

On the day Henry Ford died, Rankin brought him over to Dad's office. Rankin was Mrs. Ford's chauffeur. Wilson, Mr. Ford's driver, was probably flooded out. So Rankin waited around while Ford and Dad drove around examining the flood damage to the Village.

Then for some reason Mr. Ford took a notion to go to the Rouge plant. I don't know how they ever got there, because damn near every road leading to the Rouge was flooded. Then they returned to the estate, where the electricity was still out and heat had not yet been restored. Fireplaces were roaring to take out the dampness.

Mrs. Ford was worried about that day's dinner, and she gave Dad a turkey to take home for our Japanese cook, Sato—formerly the Ford cook—to prepare and then bring back for their dinner. Dad eventually got back with the turkey, and Sato did his best with it.

The last meal that Ford ate was that turkey dinner. Earlier Mother had taken over a veal roast for their lunch.

Dad went to bed early, and later in the evening Mother received a call on the private line—all Bell phones had gone dead much earlier. It was one of the Ford servants, sounding hysterical. "Mrs. Ford said to call you. She thinks he's dying. Hurry! Call the doctor, and come right away."

As we reconstructed the story later, Ford had eaten dinner early and gone to bed. He had awakened coughing. He had called Mrs. Ford, and Mrs. Ford had sent a maid to get him a glass of water.

The coughing subsided, and Ford lay down and rested. Then they noticed that his breathing was labored. In about an hour or so he was near death, and they called us.

Mother said, "Send someone to the plant to call Doctor Mateer, and I'll try from here. I'll be right there."

Mother shouted up to Dad, and while he was getting dressed, she phoned me to meet them at Fairlane. Fortunately she knew that I was at my usual haunt—Meyers' Seafood—having a late dinner.

Knowing that it would take me half an hour in my Ford wagon to backtrack around the flood, I headed for the experimental garage and grabbed a jeep. Fortunately, it was only five blocks from the restaurant. I got to Fairlane in a matter of minutes, but it was too late. Even as I entered the foyer, I could sense that he had died.

Today the tour guides taking tourists through Fairlane have it wrong. They say Ford was on the sun porch, but I saw him in bed with his head cocked to the right and with his eyes partly open. After I came downstairs, a good half-hour passed before Dr. John Mateer and Henry II and his wife Anne arrived.

Henry had driven as fast as he could from Grosse Pointe. Mrs. Ford was taking it relatively calmly, sitting in the library with her head bowed as if in prayer. I stayed until the body was removed; I watched him leave Fairlane for the last time.

It was the end of an era. He had ushered in the modern age, and now he was bowing out, without fuss or fanfare. So typical. I'm sure it was exactly his kind of death.

15
Good-by, Henry Ford

I have said many things about Henry Ford, but there is so much more to say. Since our paths will not cross again except in this, my first and only book, I want to bring him back to life just once more for you, the reader, to see him as I saw him.

My memory of him is usually how he was in our old farm-house, before we moved into the grand manor that was part of what is still called the Dahlinger estate. I see him now in his favorite chair, in which he liked to catch a little nap. There was a small pillow in the chair, which Mother had given him. As one of their private jokes, he would make a little ritual of plumping it and arranging it to fit the small of his back. It was a family chuckle that five minutes after he had gotten it all arranged to suit himself, the pillow would be on the floor next to the chair. Mother laughed and teased him, saying, "You see, you can handle an empire but you can't handle a pillow. Now, *I* can do both."

I'm sure he believed her. Almost. He did have faith in women and what they could talk men into, but he didn't have faith in their ability to run a company—or a country.

He was most annoyed that FDR had chosen a woman to head the Labor Department—Frances Perkins. And he refused to have any dealings with her, although she was always sending him nice messages and pleading with him to do this or that, like be nice to the unions.

On the other hand, a woman had dreamed up the Peace Ship and that had led to fame beyond his wildest dreams, and the possibility of his becoming a senator. Or president. So women were aces high there. And a "right-thinking woman"—far right of center, that is—had struck his fancy with a book called *Red Network*, and he financed her trip to Europe to find out more about the "Red menace."

So to that extent, he liked women.

And, oh yes. He said he liked children because they were so honest.

Now for what he hated.

He hated just about everything else. FDR was about first on his list. And after that what he called "monied" Jews, and all those he even suspected of admiring the monied Jews. And Catholics. He felt they were not much better.

I remember when his eldest grandson was marrying and converted to Catholicism, Henry Ford almost had a heart attack at our place. It was as though he had been stabbed. He seemed oblivious to the fact that Mother, his own beloved, was also Catholic. But that was Henry Ford.

And though he hated Jews in theory, he truly loved Izzy Strub, a local storekeeper, and I can see them now cackling away like two cronies over a cracker barrel in a general store.

And I remember target practice with Mother and Henry Ford. I am holding a .22 pistol. I can almost see it now—the .22, the target range, the slim, ramrod-straight Ford, looking so tall next to petite Evangeline.

I see the special post that was installed so bullets couldn't ricochet, and the bales of straw so the bullets couldn't go anywhere.

I am suddenly smiling as I see everyone with a gun—Harry Bennett, Dad, Mother, Ford's driver. I remember the time Ford had a .38 in his belt. Sometimes he didn't bother to carry a gun, because everyone else was in charge of protecting him.

In his later years, Ford's driving was hilarious. If he decided to turn left he turned left. Let the people behind be damned.

If I thought he was going to take the wheel, I would say, "Mr. Ford, why don't you let me drive?" and I would slide into the driver's seat, hardly giving him a chance to decide.

When he ventured out alone in a car, one of the Ford people would immediately jump into a chase car, following and acting as interference from the rear. Ford would get furious as hell and tell Dad to fire the man who had followed him.

Of course the man had only been doing what he had been told; so, instead, Dad would have him transferred to another location that Mr. Ford did not frequent.

How time flies! I can see the tree house at Fairlane where today's generation of Ford executives played with me when we were all children together. But by the time they reached their teens, they had their own friends in the Pointe, and their visits to their grandparents became, it seemed to me, fewer and further apart—maybe a stop in on a Sunday.

They were dating and having lives of their own. Then they were marrying. Bill Ford acquired the Detroit Lions football team, a switch from tennis.

Henry II was divorced from Anne McDonnell and married the international glamor girl Cristina Austin, but eventually broke up with her as well.

My wife ran into Cristina Ford when they both went backstage to say hello to George Hamilton after a performance of *Star-Spangled Girl*. George came over to greet Bette, and introduced her to the others in the cast.

When Cristina heard the name Dahlinger, she quickly turned and took a surprised look at Bette. It was clear to my wife that the name rang a discordant bell with her.

The only Fords who ever came to my supper club were Bill and Josephine.

Now and then I would see Benson. I could especially count on running into him over the three weekends of the Indianapolis time trials and race. We'd sit around the bar and discuss the various cars and drivers—nothing too intimate.

Memories flood back. Ford wearing long johns summer and winter. It wasn't so strange—so did Dad. They wore lighter-weight ones for summer.

Ford enjoyed earning money, and he also enjoyed spending it. He warned me to remember that money was "just a commodity." Money in itself did not thrill Ford; it was what he could do with it. I believe he kept several million dollars in cash so that he could do new things whenever he wanted to, without going through the company and doing a lot of paper-work.

I remember one of the jokes around the plant was that Henry Ford had sent John D. Rockefeller an automobile as a present, and Rockefeller had sent him a dime.

I wondered aloud why Rockefeller passed out dimes to all the children he met and was told that when the tycoon would give the dime, he would say, "Young man, that is the interest on a dollar in a year. Make it work for you."

I can see Ford now, moving rapidly, always in action—bounding up stairs, on his bicycle, on his skates, striding rapidly as if he hadn't a minute to lose.

If Mother or I complained about the weather, Ford always took the side of the weather. "Well, you can't change the weather," he would say, "so you'd better change your attitude toward it."

Sometimes he would try to trick me into saying some other car was better than a Ford, but I never would. He seemed most worried about the Chevrolet, and he would drill and drill me in comparing each part of the motor and body of the two cars. But I would never tell him that a Chevrolet was better than a Ford, because I didn't ever think it was.

Henry Ford liked to wear a hat. Even in summer he would wear a flat, stiff-brimmed straw hat. Other men wore soft panamas, but Mr. Ford liked a stiff hat.

He was pretty particular about his suits. He would order several at a time and be done for another season. But he didn't have much variety: gray tweed, gray check, solid gray. He'd have some formal wear for dancing, and a dinner jacket.

Ford didn't patronize the local tailors. He went to a tailor he called Sima. He did have a first name, Frank. Sima's shop was in Ypsilanti—a short distance from Dearborn. But Sima always came to Mr. Ford. He was Dad's and my tailor as well.

Every now and then Ford would become philosophical and ponder the meaning of life and why people were put on earth. From what he told me, he felt destined to improve the world in many ways, and he fought time to accomplish all he set out to do.

He wanted from earliest childhood to do away with grueling farm work, and he helped accomplish some of that with the tractor.

He wanted the poor man to have something that would put him on a par with the rich man, and he did this with the automobile.

He believed that substitutes for expensive materials like iron, steel, and rubber could come from the most humble plants that a farmer could grow, and he made great strides in ushering in the plastic age.

Quite a list of accomplishments for one man.

After Ford died, things were never the same for Mother or Dad. There was immediately danger of Dad's being kicked out—as most of Ford's cronies were. But Mrs. Ford insisted that she needed Ray Dahlinger.

Dad had his job, but he was a lost soul without his old guiding light. And almost the moment Mrs. Ford died in 1950, Dad's office was locked. He was crushed, because he had many valuable mementos of his forty-four years with the company and of Henry Ford that he wanted to preserve. He had thought of giving many of the things to the Ford Museum. But now he didn't have the chance. The key had been turned.

He rescued what he could, but he grieved till the end of his days about the destruction of his treasures and the relics of his fondest memories. He died in 1969. As we understand it, most of these valuable mementos were taken to the dump and destroyed.

When Mr. Ford died, I was told he had between $26 and $28 million in the bank. This is not counting whatever money was in both safes.

Unfortunately, these were not the early days, and now several other people besides Mother and Dad had the combinations. Once Mother had been a little upset when someone stopped by to see her as he was leaving the company and showed her a suitcase full of money, saying it was a million dollars.

If it was true, it presumably involved an arrangement with Mr. Ford, a private matter that didn't concern her. She had a right to be a little upset, however, because Mr. Ford also had an arrangement with her and Dad that if anything happened to him, what remained in the safe was theirs.

Obviously Ford was playing both ends against the middle. I believe Dad asked Ford what had happened and Ford said that the other person was entitled to something, too. When Ford died, the safe to which Mother and Dad and others had the combination was empty.

There is a mystery about Ford's will and a certain codicil to it that may never be solved.

As I recall, I heard much conversation about Henry Ford's horror lest the company which he had worked so hard to build go public. He wanted to ensure that all stock would remain in the hands of family members for at least ten years after his death.

I was told many times that Ford had called in Cappie—his lawyer, I. A. Capizzi—and told him to draw up a codicil saying that a half-dozen or so men from the old regime would be members of the board. Dad would be one, and so would Cappie, Charles Lindbergh, Charles Sorensen, and Harry Bennett, the latter being in charge of labor relations.

Henry Ford showed the codicil around, and Henry II somehow or other got wind of it and got very excited. By its provisions, Henry II could be kept from being anything but a token president, as his father had been, for ten years after his grandfather's death. The Tooth and his mother went to see Mr. and Mrs. Henry Ford and, according to the story I heard, told them that if Ford didn't rescind the codicil, they would sell their stock on the open market.

There are several versions of what happened to the codicil. One is that Harry Bennett burned a copy of the codicil in front of John Bugas, a former FBI man considered to be an informant for the Tooth.

He burned it, the story went, so that Bugas would go back to Henry II and say that it had been taken care of and that the codicil was no more.

Dad believed that Henry Ford had signed the original and that Bennett only had an unsigned copy of the original. He said Bennett burned the copy so that Henry II would be confident it would never get to Ford to be signed. Henry II did not know, Dad said, that Henry Ford had the original folded up in his wallet. In fact, Dad claimed he saw the signed codicil after Bennett had left the company. It was still with Henry Ford.

Where is the codicil and what happened to the original? Capizzi, I believe, said that the codicil had never been witnessed and so it was not a legal document, but knowing Henry Ford, I am sure it could have been witnessed by a servant without Capizzi's knowledge.

Bennett was fired shortly after he supposedly got rid of the codicil in 1945, and Dad remained unworried, secure in the belief that there was another copy somewhere.

When Ford trusted someone, he went all the way; he would

sign his name and even get his wife to sign her name to a document to be filled out later. For example, when Henry Ford was giving the folks the estate I now live on, he did this with the deed to the land on which the house was built. He signed it and got his wife to sign it, but just exactly how much land the folks were getting was left blank. Mother and Dad could have written in the Rouge plant had they wanted to.

Actually, it was years before the oversight was discovered and a new deed was made up. But knowing how tricky Ford could be and how he tried to shoulder expenses for Mother, it was quite possible that Ford knew exactly what he was doing and was trying to spare the folks from having to pay taxes on the property, which they would have had to do had it been filled in.

The important thing about the codicil is that had it gone into effect, Henry II would not have been in full charge of the company until ten years after Ford's death.

Did persons unknown destroy the codicil? Dad never was a part of the company board, and Bennett was no longer a part of the company. Within a few years, shortly after Mrs. Ford died in 1950, Henry Ford's worst fears were realized: the company did indeed go public.

Henry Ford would probably turn over in his grave if he knew that the Ford Motor Company had sold its stock on the open market. I don't know how many times I heard him talk about how he planned to protect his family and grandchildren by making sure the company would always be a family affair, and about how I was protected, too. Mr. Ford said that Dad would be on the board of trustees by the time John—meaning me—would be ready to become a part of the company, and Dad could just work me into a proper position. Mr. Ford never realized that I had other plans.

As soon as Ford was dead, Mother was "retired" from the company. She still did all the things she had done for Mrs. Ford, but now as a friend, not an employee.

Good-by, Henry Ford

When Mrs. Ford died on September 27, 1950, the Dahlingers' careers at Ford died too.

I spend my time at the Dahlinger estate, as usual, and at the lake, in our summer home on the Huron. At the lake, I still walk over to the windmill and look inside and remember nostalgically how excited I used to get when the famous pilot, Harry Brooks, would come to stay at the windmill. He loved it there and thought a windmill was the perfect place to live.

Other than the fact that I am writing this book, nothing has changed much. Caretakers are still protecting the properties, especially when I retreat now and then to the north woods. Every so often I dabble in real estate.

I still go to the Dearborn Country Club, where I play golf and shoot the breeze with the old Ford gang, none of whom know that I finally decided to write this book. There are some things one must do alone.

I don't know much about my old playmates. When I was old enough to go to the academy, I lost track of the Ford grandchildren. They showed no interest in continuing our childhood. friendships. It would be a safe bet that Mother's relationship with their grandfather had something to do with it.

But at our house we were getting all the family scuttlebutt as usual, from their grandpa Henry himself. When Henry II married Anne McDonnell, Henry Ford was fit to be tied, because she had gotten young Henry to convert to Catholicism. He was like a man possessed.

He had a sudden inspiration as to how he could express his displeasure: he decided to go through all the steps of Masonry to become a thirty-third-degree Mason. This was in June 1940; I was seventeen at the time of Henry II's wedding.

I thought it was a nice touch that Edsel Ford gave his son a gift of 25,000 shares of Ford stock. Edsel also gave a little speech at the wedding which was probably aimed more at Henry Ford than at the guests.

He was transferring the stock to young Henry, he said, "in recognition of the fact that you are finishing your college career this month, and after being married will join the Ford Motor Company as your future business, and also because of the fact that you are at the present time a director of the company."

In spite of the way he felt about the bride's religion, Henry Ford danced with her, and judging from a newspaper picture of the event that I found in Mother's collection, he seemed to enjoy it very much.

Within a few months, the next grandchild, Benson, became engaged to Edith McNaughton, daughter of the Lynn McNaughtons of Grosse Pointe. This fact is important because again Henry Ford was miserable. McNaughton was a high executive with the Cadillac Motor Company. But good-hearted Benson paid his grandfather no mind and got married in July 1941.

I don't remember exactly when the younger grandchildren got married. William Clay Ford married Martha Firestone. Josephine married an interior designer, whose name, by sheer coincidence, was also Ford—Walter Buhl Ford, whose family was connected with Wyandotte Chemicals.

For a lot of people, it was a bad day when Henry II stepped into his grandfather's shoes and cleaned house. Almost everyone even remotely associated with his grandfather was fired, dismissed, retired with several years' continuance on the payroll in absentia, or insulted into quitting.

Dad was one of the few who held on, because Mrs. Ford counted on him for those important little things like checking her rose gardens and making sure her case of Cherry Heering was ordered and her beer was delivered by the truckload—she believed in stocking up for a long period of time.

Henry II did get rid of my three uncles, who were dealers and who had been rather successful at training some of the better dealers in the business.

He got rid of them by using a very simple technique. When

his grandfather died, he simply demanded various things that were financially impossible—that they make various improvements on their buildings and that they maintain a huge inventory of cars that they could not possibly sell. Consequently they all sold out.

Evidently, as the twig is bent, so grows the tree. As a result of constantly talking cars with Henry Ford, I started reading automobile magazines as soon as I became aware of them. I still read *Car and Driver, Road and Track, Motor Trend, Auto Week, Automobile Quarterly,* and *The World of Automobiles,* a fancy cover deal. I also collect model cars. Furthermore, I still build model cars, and I never fail to think of Ford as I tinker with them.

In the last few years of Henry Ford's life, Mother no longer kept her diary, but Ray Dahlinger did keep his. And I'm glad, because his is the only exact account we have of the day that Henry Ford died and the days that immediately followed.

Just before Ford died, he had gone on vacation with Mrs. Ford to their home in Ways, Georgia. According to Dad's diary, they had phoned him to come down and join them at Richmond Hill.

It is interesting to note the flow of events leading to Henry Ford's last day. (Incidentally, the New Deal refers not to FDR's administration, but to Henry II's new regime at the Ford Motor Company. As mentioned before, "Bill" was Dad's name for Mother. Other first names refer to servants.)

Thursday, January 16 [1947]

To work at 9:00. Mrs. Ford wanted to see me about Railroad car and shipping goods to Ways. Talked about three quarters of an hour. Talked to Henry the second about the folks and about Mrs. Ford's cars. He said he would help to get them fixed. But he said he left it up to me. He was OK today. Mr. and Mrs. Ford leaving January 25. Boss not so good, hope he gets better.

Friday, January 17

Henry Ford called to tell me about cars he will have me get for Richmond Hill. Talked to Mrs. Ford about when help was to leave for Ways. She will tell me Monday.

Monday, January 20

Got to work at 8:30. Got turkey for Mrs. Ford, hope it was ok. Boss not so good, so sorry. Hope he gets better!

Tuesday, January 21

To work at 9:30. Getting ready for the help and Mr. and Mrs. Ford to go to Richmond Hill. Lots of work, too many bosses. Hope everything will be ok. Boss not too good.

Friday, January 24

Had date with Mrs. Ford. Looked at all beds and chairs she is going to give to Henry for his new house. Mrs. Ford was fine. So was boss.

Saturday, February 1

To work at 9:30. Stayed around farm—went to office at ten o'clock. Moved cars to Mr. Ford's garage till they come back. The new deal is working to get us out of the plant. Hope we can stay and have my office there till we move all my junk home. Home at 4:30. Stayed home, listened to the radio, and Bill and I played with the dogs.

Wednesday, February 5

To work at 9:30. Stayed around office till 2:00, made rounds. Very cold. Not so good. New deal is stepping right in. Hope it will be O.K. and I will stay and help them. April 15, I will be with FMC 44 years.

Monday, February 10

To work at 9:30. Made rounds. To office at 10:30. Truman

mad at me. Too many people telling things I never say. Too much back-stabbing.

Monday, February 17

Went over to the boss's house, talked to John and Fritz and went through the power house. Mrs. Ford called at four thirty— gave orders and asked me if I could come to Richmond Hill. The Boss wants me. Hope I can make it and the boss is O.K.

Monday, February 24

Talked to Mrs. Ford. She wants me to come to Richmond Hill to talk to Mr. Ford. He wants me to come down. I cannot go till Tuesday March 4th. Hope plane will be ready.

Tuesday, February 25

To work at 9:30. Stayed at office until 2:00. The weather here is cold. Not too warm at Richmond Hill. Talked to Waddell. He said Mrs. Ford wants me to come to Richmond Hill.

Thursday, February 27

To work at 9:30. Stayed at office till 2:00. Went to Will Run and made rounds. New deal working hard to get us.

Tuesday, March 4

To plant at 9:00. The boys are loading plane. Got lots of food and things for Mrs. Ford. Plane ready at 10:00, left Dearborn at 11:20, arrived at 3:20 and Richmond Hill at 5:00.

Wednesday, March 5

Talked to Mr. and Mrs. Ford at 7:00 Tuesday. Had a good breakfast and dinner and supper. Made the rounds with Newman and Ross. Mr. and Mrs. Ford and I went to colored school. Mrs. Ford checking. She is right. Too much spending.

Thursday, March 6

To Cherry Hill at 9:30. Made rounds with Newman and Ross.

Mrs. Ford wants me to fix up the old Fort. Big job. Going to take Whitey to check the job. Took Mr. Ford for a ride. Went to Gills for steaks and had a good time. But he wouldn't let me pay.

March 7

Home

Monday, March 10

To work at 9:00. Talked to Waddell. He said Mrs. Ford wants me to come to Richmond Hill again, before they come North. The New Deal is working to get us all on other jobs. Miss Lynch is pretty sick—Mrs. D. up there for the last three days.

Monday, March 17

To work at 9:30. Stayed at office till 2:15. Made rounds. Then went to see pony for Henry II for his little girl. Got to have pony by April 3rd. I looked at one that I think will do. She's a beauty! Mr. and Mrs. Ford going to come home about March 30. New Deal checking on us.

Tuesday, March 18

To work at 9:30. Bought Sandy, spotted pony for Henry II's little girl. He looks good to me. I'm sure she'll love it.

Wednesday, March 19

To work at 9:30. Went to the barn to see the pony work—checked him out. He is a fine pony, he looks good and is very gentle. Waddell called and said Mr. and Mrs. Ford want me to come to Richmond Hill to see them Monday, March 24th.

Thursday, March 20

Talked to Waddell—he said Boss said for me to come to Richmond Hill. Mrs. Ford said she had the best time this year. Everything seemed to be O.K.

Good-by, Henry Ford

Saturday, March 22

Left 10:30 in Ford's DC-3. Arrived in 3 hours and 18 minutes. Talked with Mr. and Mrs. Ford about the Fort.

Sunday, March 23

Got up at 7:30, had breakfast at eight o'clock. Talked with Mr. and Mrs. Ford, then Rankin, Mrs. Ford's chauffeur, and I made the rounds. Lunch with Mr. and Mrs. Ford at 12:30. Weather warm.

Monday, March 24

Saw Mr. and Mrs. Ford. Had long talk about the Fort and Ford Motor Company. Got O.K. to start work on the Fort. A Big Job! Mr. and Mrs. Ford left for Rome 7:45. We had to stay— bad weather.

Sunday, March 30

Mr. and Mrs. Ford got in at Smith Creek depot at 9:30. They looked good. Mrs. Ford is a Doctor (honorary doctorate). Well, she worked hard for it, but it will cost a lot of money. Got home about 11:00 and had breakfast, then to the barn to talk about the horses we are going to race.

Monday, March 31

The folks came home from the South, Sunday, March 30th at 9:30. They say they had the best time they ever had. Everything was just fine and no trouble with the help or the farms. That's something to be proud of. Those were Mr. and Mrs. Ford's exact words. She said that I made it all possible.

Thursday, April 3rd

To work at 9:30, stayed at office till 2:00. Made the rounds with Schroder. Henry II called and said not to bring the pony—his little girl has a cold.

Friday, April 4th

To office at 10:00. Have a little cold so stayed home till 9:30. Henry II called and said to bring pony, his little girl was better. The children were glad and liked the pony. Mrs. Ford said she wanted six horse truck to take pony and load for the east. We will be ready.

Sunday, April 6

Rain, rain, rain, the water is going up. It is in the boss's place. All lights and heat gone. Hope the Boss and Mrs. do not get too cold. I have all the men working to get the place cleaned up. It is the worst rain in years. Hope Boss will be O.K.

Monday, April 7

Mrs. Ford wants me to come to the house. She had Mrs. D. send lunch over from our house. Had veal and Mrs. Ford said it was good. Mrs. Ford gave me a turkey that she got from Rome. Had it cooked and took it to her home at 6:15. Boss and Mrs. O.K. Talked to Boss at 10:00 a.m., he was fine. Mr. Ford came to office with Rankin and I talked to him. He said he wanted me Tuesday to make rounds with him. I just cannot get it. Bill called me and said the Boss died at 11:45. Stayed with Mr. and Mrs. Ford. Mrs. Ford taking it all right. Hope she will not break down. I cannot believe Mr. Ford is dead. The world is taking it badly. I just cannot see. I lost my best friend.

And somehow life went on:

Wednesday, April 9

Stayed at the office all day. Went to see Mr. Ford with Rich Kroll. We can not believe we lost our best friend. There were eighty thousand people to see Mr. Ford today. We were the last ones to see Mr. Ford.

Thursday, April 10

Stayed around until twelve-thirty. Had to make lunch for

twenty people. I am very sad. Hope everything will be okay and the New Deal will leave me alone to run the Farms. Hope Mrs. Ford sticks with us.

Friday, April 11

To work at nine-thirty. The place is like a boat without a rudder. I am going to miss the boss. It's a sad thing and hard to believe.

Saturday, April 12

To the office at ten o'clock. Not many at work. The new men are no damn good. Hope Henry II will get wise to them.

Sunday, April 13

Stayed home 'til ten-thirty. Went to the plant then to see Mr. Ford's grave. Drove horses.

Monday, April 14

To work at nine-thirty. Stayed at office 'til two-thirty, then took flowers to Mr. Ford's grave. I can not believe he is gone. My best friend is gone. We will all miss him. Mrs. Ford is standing up good. She said she is very tired.

Tuesday, April 15

Hope things will be okay. We will have been here 44 years today.

Thursday, April 17

Met Fritz, made rounds, and went to Cherry Hill. But there is something missing. It's Mr. Ford. He was a great man.

Friday, April 18

To office at eight-thirty. Mrs. Ford wanted me. She looks tired. Too much company. We had a long talk. I will do all I can to help Mrs. Ford. I know that is the way Mr. Ford would want it. We all miss him so.

Monday, June 9

To office at nine-thirty. Stayed there and village 'til five-thirty. Very warm and a lot of people in village. Don Grant and Charles Piper came out to see me about watchman at Mr. Ford's cemetery. They think it costs too much. That's a new one. Well, it's the new deal.

Thursday, June 19

To office at nine o'clock. Mrs. Ford called. She wanted me in Village at ten o'clock. Stayed with Mrs. Ford until eleven-thirty. She wanted me to change the chair in the Lincoln courthouse. She was very good.

Friday, June 20

To office at nine-thirty. Mrs. Ford going to Billy Ford's wedding. Mrs. Ford looked good. I hope she can take it.

Sunday, June 22

Stayed home 'til one-thirty. Went to the Village at two o'clock and stayed 'til three. Went home and dressed to meet Mrs. Ford. Took her to the Village and stayed 'til five o'clock. Mrs. Ford looked good. Home at six-thirty.

Thursday, July 10

To the office at nine. Mrs. Ford and I went to check boat for August first and second. I will meet her Saturday and take her to the Village.

Saturday, July 12

Met Mrs. Ford and we went to the Village at ten o'clock. Mrs. Ford and I went through many buildings. She said she wanted a live Village, not a dead one and she said she could bring back three pair of horses and instructed us to start building.

Friday, July 18

To office at nine o'clock. Saw Mrs. Ford at nine-thirty. Talked about Village. She said the men taking care of the house were to be under my jurisdiction. Also, the Village is to be a live one. Peacock House to be started at once.

Saturday, August 2

Mrs. Ford . . . left for Huron Mountain Club at one-thirty. Mrs. Ford feeling very bad. Boat looks very dirty. Hope Mrs. Ford has a good time.

Tuesday, August 5

John tried to fly Mrs. Ford's order to Big Bay but the weather was bad.

Thursday, September 4

To the office at 9:00. Mrs. Ford wanted me to go to the Village with her. Hard job ahead. John came in with his new plane.

When Dad died in 1969 at the age of eighty-three, there were no condolences from the Ford Motor Company or any member of the family. But someone must have been aware of his death, because his retirement checks stopped.

There is no doubt that Henry Ford tried to provide for Mother and me before he died. In fact, she and Mr. D. had an argument sometime before Mr. Ford died. Ford had given her a blank check out of his checkbook. The check was signed by Henry Ford, and the date was left blank.

Dad was angry and confronted her with the check. Mother tore it up with a "so there" attitude.

I do not know how long Mother had the check or how Mr. D. found out about it—or what the check was for. Was it simply a gift for her to spend as she liked, or was it connected with my birth? It was not the kind of thing Mother would talk about, and I have not yet run across anything in her papers that would solve the mystery.

But it would be typical of Mr. Ford to have done such a thing. Later, Mother frequently spoke with regret of having torn up the blank check that Henry Ford had given her, because the Ford family seemed very uncaring.

Sometime after Henry Ford died, a Fairlane group which was worried about what was happening to the historic Ford home wanted Mother to come over and restore the rose garden to the way she had known it.

Henry Ford Museum also wanted Mother to record her memories of Mr. Ford so that they could be preserved, but Mother told them it had been a personal and private relationship and she did not wish to share it with the world.

Henry Ford had told my Mother that when I got out of the service he wanted me to choose a factory I wanted to head. This was in 1942 or 1943, not long before Edsel died. It was obvious that Henry Ford was never quite the same man after Edsel died: he probably felt a great guilt for the rest of his life.

As long as she lived, Edsel's wife, Eleanor, faithfully supplied money to the Art Institute in memory of her husband. But she was so modest that when she donated a million dollars for the construction of a new wing in 1962, she refused to let the wing be named after her husband. Personally, I was sorry; I felt that Edsel Ford should have been honored this way.

And just as Edsel had brought great Mexican art to the institute, Eleanor brought a great Italian masterpiece to the institute: *The Conversion of the Magdalene*. It was a long-lost sixteenth-century painting by Michelangelo Merisi da Caravaggio and cost well over a million dollars.

When Eleanor Ford died in October 1976, she was one of the richest women in the world.

On one of my last visits to Mr. Ford, he was out on his sun porch, looking much older and more subdued than I had ever seen him.

It almost choked me up when he said, as I was leaving, "Don't get married too soon, John. Have some fun first." It was almost as if he were talking about himself, realizing he had never taken time just to be a young man having fun. He had been earning a living since he was fifteen.

It's difficult to explain my feelings as I finish my memoirs of Henry Ford. Relief is my first emotion; it has been so long that I have kept my secrets. I have pooh-poohed the secret of my paternity for years to keep people off my back and to keep them from embarrassing my mother.

When I married Bette, I told her to use my old line when people tried to probe: "If you can prove it, we'll split an empire with you."

But now the game is over, and I'm glad. And I want to say a few words in praise of Mr. Ford's treatment of me. Given the mores of the early '20s, the years when I was growing up, he did the right thing. I'm sure he made it a much easier life for Mother and me. It was relatively scandal-free; whisper-filled, perhaps, but scandal-free, at least as far as the newspapers were concerned.

He might not have made waves by publicly acknowledging me, but at least he didn't sweep me under the rug. He made a friend of me. For this I salute him.

Index